LEADERSHIP
AND
HORSES

DON JESSOP – Mastery Horsemanship

WWW.MASTERYHORSEMANSHIP.COM

Editors: Allison Jessop and MJ Schwader
Interior Design and Layout: Rachel Jessop

ISBN-13: 978-0-9827305-2-2
ISBN-10: 0982730527

Library of Congress Control Number: 2017906983

Dedication

I dedicate this book to Legacy.
The memory of your patient and willing spirit burns deep inside me.

Acknowledgments

My wife Rachel, for your inspirational horse mastery skills and never-ending love and support.

My daughter Shona, for your sweet, genuine, curious nature, and willingness to try anything.

My lifelong friend Joe, for your brotherhood in all my life decisions.

Ingela and Richard for their friendship and wisdom and encouragement over the years. *(Ingela is a master with horses and she is featured many times throughout this book and has contributed many great photos to support us.)*

Christina Hirst, for her friendship, authenticity, and fantastic photos.

My precious Legacy, who's touched the lives of countless people and remains in the caring hands of two great friends, Lisa and Jess.

And ALL the horses around the world who have taught me the truth of your experiences in my human hands.

My siblings and parents, for your free form encouragement, generosity, and kindness. Special thanks to my brother Ben for bringing horses into my life.

Pat and Linda Parelli, for their undying love to educate horse people.

John Lyons, Monty Roberts, Ray Hunt, Walter Zettle, Tom Dorrance, Buck Brannaman, Mikey and Wally, Rob, Mel, Steve, Andy, Ronnie, Aimee, Karen, Honza, Kaffa, Alan, Neil, Stephanie, Carmen, Reid, and all the other horsemen and women who have influenced my career in personal and positive ways.

Photo credit goes to:

Christina Hirst
Ingela Larsson Smith
The Brazil Horses for Orphans Team
Coco Baptist
Matt & Jen DeLong
Carrie Maier
Mandy Mcarthur
Sonja Rasche
Rebecca Harris
Anwar Sher
Claire Spelling
& of course, all of the fabulous horse talent…

Acknowledgments - Horses for Orphans

My good friends Ingela and Richard Larsson Smith travel the world sharing the love of God through the experience of horses and leadership training courses with orphans. Their vision is one I fully support, and a percentage of proceeds from each book will be donated to help them continue their work.

Special Note: Many of the young adults Ingela and Richard work with through the Horses for Orphan's projects are featured in this book. You'll notice they aren't wearing helmets or boots, but remain fearless in their learning and safe with a master by their side. They have the heart and desire to accomplish beautiful things.

Learn more at www.horsesfororphans.com

Table of Contents

Important Safety Note and Disclaimer

Horses, even small ones, outweigh most humans. They're faster, stronger, and in some cases, more reactive. As a result, people can and do get hurt and even die working with horses. Horses can also get hurt and die during human interactions. The information in this book won't ever change that fact. The contents here can merely guide your mind to think differently and to see horses and leadership from a new perspective. With time, practice, and professional support you will become better at reading horse behavior and preparing for more successful encounters. However, because safety is a priority, wearing safety gear such as a helmet and boots while interacting with horses is highly recommend. Always keep safety in mind as you venture out into the pasture to be with horses.

The content, authors, editors, and publishers of this book do not claim any responsibility for your personal safety with horses. You alone can do that.

Prepare well and stay out of danger. The techniques introduced throughout this book may help you prepare mentally, but cannot keep you from danger. You must seek the support from qualified professionals if you feel inadequate in any way around horses.

Important Note about Training Techniques

In my 20 years of teaching, training, and consulting in the horse industry, one thing has always stood out to me: people tend to make rules about how things have to be done. People buy into techniques and programs. Don't make the assumption that there is only one way to do things. Keep an open mind as you read and don't turn techniques into rules! Keep your focus on principles instead. Follow the programs. Use the techniques you've been given, but stay alerted to other techniques. A good leader is always open to learning. A follower closes all other doors and does what the leader says. When it comes to horsemanship, you want to be a good leader, not a follower!

INTRODUCTION

Horses have been an integral part of human lives for as long as we can record. In the beginning, horses were more than likely used primarily as a source of food for hunters. As time passed, the value of the horse changed and hunters began to see how they could be used for farming or transportation. Warriors also saw their value for speed, strength, and endurance on, to, and from the battlefield. And then came industry: roads, canals, logging, construction, etc. Horses have been a form of status and power, providing the people who were fortunate the ability to do and create more than ever before. But the focus and value of the horse has changed once again. Now, the horse is used primarily for recreation and entertainment. There are a few cultures remaining that rely heavily on horses for industry, and some cultures even rely on them for food; but most merely want horses for the *feeling* they give us – for the value of entertainment.

Because of this most recent change in value, humans interacting fairly with animals is paramount. Fairness was always important, but now it has become critical. With horses, we've always had a special responsibility to provide their basic survival needs: water, food, and shelter in exchange for their labor. Under close examination, however, providing those needs alone does not help a horse thrive, especially because we don't provide them with a sense of industry and purpose any more. That being said… we, the horse owners, **must** become better leaders. We must learn to provide the horse with meaningful interaction and avoid slave-like ownership. Without a clear purpose and positive stimuli, horses lose track of leadership and can become complacent or even dangerous. The principle is this: any captive held against his or her will *must* be compensated with positive and productive interaction, otherwise be at risk of going completely insane.

The purpose of this book is to teach horse trainers, riders, and owners to become better leaders, so that he or she can provide the horse with what it needs most, regardless of the breed or discipline the horse is being trained to undertake. The focus is to help the individual productively progress to whatever end, with the horse's mental and emotional health retained and even enhanced.

One of my goals in this book is to teach you how to become the kind of leader that can inspire confidence and trust in your horse by using what I call the Four Step Leadership Formula. I believe once you have learned and successfully applied the concepts in this book you will have the kind of horse most people "wish" they had. You will be proud of what your horse has become for you and proud of what you've become for your horse.

Confidence training will encompass the majority of this book because without a confident horse, your own confidence will wane. And when confidence deteriorates, horses lose their value. A valueless horse is doomed to suffering and ultimately, destruction. Horses easily get confused, distracted, frustrated, or scared. I want you, the owner or trainer, to be able to see what's going on and address each issue confidently, with specific strategies and technical information passed on by masterful trainers in the horse industry. If you can follow the concepts in this book regardless of the training disciplines you choose, you too can become masterful with horses and help them bravely accept and embrace everything we ask of them.

Why do you want a confident horse? What will it mean to you if you have a totally confident horse for riding or playful interactions? What if your horse could be smarter, braver, calmer, and more balanced? Would those things be valuable for you and would they be valuable for your horse?

You may have picked this book up because your horse doesn't have perfect confidence in some situations. Because of this you also may not feel safe riding. I know I don't feel comfortable riding a scared or unsafe horse. Like me, I'm sure you want to make progress toward having a better equine partner and becoming a better leader. You want to see your horse blossom and become more confident, not just for his or her sake, but yours as well. I believe the secrets written in this book will give you fantastic cutting edge techniques and tools, and a whole new perspective on leadership with your horse.

Throughout this book, you will get layer upon layer of valuable information regarding your horse's confidence, and in turn, your own. By the end you will not only know more about confidence training than most professional trainers, but you will also have a grasp on basic to advanced skill development with your horse.

I've had people all over the country ask me, "From the outside, it looks like you've got everything under control." And in reality, when it comes to riding horses, I *do* have everything under control. That's exactly why I'm so confident. I believe I can instill that same confidence to you.

Because confidence is such a dominant part of training and leadership, there are a couple of things up front I want you to know. There are two types of confidence a person can have. One is what I call "self-confidence"; the other is "environmental control confidence."

When it comes to riding horses, I don't have a ton of self-confidence, at least not compared to many reckless rodeo type riders I know who can ride anything with hair on it. I've developed a different kind of confidence by learning to read the situation and control the environment.

The important thing for you is to become good at reading each situation so you can control yourself and your horse within it. I trust my ability to read the situation at hand to ensure our safety. I also trust my horse to respond without reacting because of the training he's had. Within these pages, you will learn what it takes to read and control your environment as well.

What I call "self-confidence" is a person's ability to react quickly enough to any particular extreme situation. That person totally trusts their body to perform under pressure. For instance, if a horse started bucking, they could instinctually react with all the necessary body parts to either stick it out or bail and most likely land on their feet. I used to have this confidence. I used to have *a lot* of this confidence. But, then I lost it. I fell. I injured my head, broke my ribs, suffered a concussion, and endured months of painful recovery.

The interesting thing is I didn't lose my self-confidence on that first fall. I lost it on the third fall, the third injury, the third recovery. I began to wonder if I could handle another fall or if my head could handle one more concussion. I began to lose trust in my body's ability to react quickly enough and recover efficiently.

I began to "hate" the ground. As a kid, I loved the ground because it was the place to roll, jump, land, slide, twist, flip, skip…you name it. The ground and I had a great relationship; but after falling time after time, I started hating the ground. It didn't serve me anymore, so I feared the ground. Sure, I could use it to stand up and walk around, but I no longer wanted to be next to it or fall toward it. I imagined the ground consuming me, holding me down, and breaking my body.

Slowly but surely, I am regaining my self-confidence. And you can as well. Although self-confidence is not the focus of this book, there are a few simple things you can do to retain it or to get it back, but it takes time and practice. I've started martial arts; we spend a lot of time on the ground in those classes. I roll around on the floor at home on purpose because it helps me develop more trust in my body's ability to react quickly. But the truth is, when it comes to horses, my confidence does not reside in myself. It resides in my ability to "control the environment" and to ensure nothing will go wrong.

Sure, not having instant self-confidence keeps me from riding broncs. I used to start young horses in a five-day training process. Now I take ten days. But now I'm safer, and I'm alive and able to continue working in this fantastic profession. My horses are safer, happier, and more relaxed too. Who would have thought that "slowing down" was a good thing! Not in this world, right? Everything moves quickly. Email, phones, TV, internet, food... everything is fast. But I'm finding with horses it pays to take things a little slower.

Slowing things down gives me the ability to ensure things go the way I want them to. For instance, I don't get on a bucking horse. I train the horse not to buck before I get on it. I ensure unsafe things won't happen every single day! I don't assume the horse will ever be cured. I have tests I run through regularly with my horses to stay focused and relaxed.

There are hundreds of techniques I can give you to mirror what I do. Principally, however, it's a shift in mindset. I don't want to get hurt and I don't want my horse to get hurt, so I set it up for success. I take the time to ensure everything will be okay. One of the ways I do that is by using what I call the "4 B's of Leadership" with my horse, which I'll give to you in this book.

What this means is that my horse will learn how "not" to react when random, strange, uncomfortable, or spooky pressures all around stimulate him because he's respectful of my space, trusts that I care about him and that he won't be hurt when odd or uncomfortable things happen around him. I want him to stand still, to stay relaxed while carrying me, and confidently carry me over obstacles or through scary situations, all the while staying balanced and healthy.

I know my limits and I test them on the ground. I follow the formula I'm going to give you and never stray from it. This religious dedication to progress keeps me alive and safe and my horses grow in their confidence rapidly. My leadership increases and as a result my horses respond better in any given situation.

What I want to do in this book is give you that four-step leadership formula in complete detail, while clearly outlining the three goals of confidence training. There is so much more... including seven clever strategies to build confidence, and many more strategies to work through common pitfalls.

I want you to become the leader your horse deserves! I want to share all these concepts with you so you can be successful and so you don't have to get hurt. You will also find that after you've worked through many of the concepts here in this book, your horse will be able to think more clearly in our human world instead of reacting instinctually to discomfort. He or she will be happier, healthier, less distracted, and safer. The way we're going to start this story is by outlining a few leadership principles. After all, we are the horse's leader and friend.

THE NINE LEADERSHIP PRINCIPLES

Before you can learn the four leadership steps or 4 B's, as I often call them, you need to first understand the nine principles of leadership with horses! These nine principles give us the foundation for how we need to act as horse owners, trainers, or riders, in order to guide our equine friends.

Principle #1: The Leader Serves

There are many models of leadership to contemplate when training horses. We could think of a parent and child or a boss and employee. We could think of a teacher and student or a coach and athlete. We could even think of a master and servant or master and slave.

Using the right model is important because if we don't, we'll mistreat the animal or the situation. In my seminars, I teach that we want to avoid **master/slave** relationships. However, even today we see slave-like horse training all over the world. People are treating their horses like motorcycles, pushing and pulling without any regard for the raw emotions of the horse. This is abuse!

Master/servant is slightly better than master/slave, but still has negative connotations. In reality though, most people in the world treat their horses like a servant with little regard for real bonding and friendship. Horses survive this kind of treatment, but don't really thrive.

The **boss/employee** model has served men and women for thousands of years. Literally, horses have been our employees doing work for us in the form of cattle management, carriage driving, pony express, and more. This model still holds up in today's world, but has the same negative connotation as the master/servant model because the horse never really chose to be our employee and the compensation for the work he does for us is minimal.

The **coach/athlete** model is a more useful model for horse training. As a coach, we want the best for our athlete. A coach measures progress as well as stress levels, notices limitations, and promotes potential. An athlete, on the other hand, wants to perform and improve. I like this model except for one small inconsistency: most horses didn't choose to be our athletes. We chose them to be our athletes. Although this model is useful, it isn't complete.

The **teacher/student** model holds the most credibility so far. In most cases, especially pre-college, we can relate to the student model. Kids don't go to school because they want to. They go because they are sent there. However, a good teacher can make a kid feel like he or she "wants" to be there. In this same way, horses didn't choose to learn with us, but a good teacher can really help that horse feel great about being there.

The remaining model is the **parent/child**, which closely resembles the teacher/student model. The child did not choose to come into this world, but he or she is here and the parent loves and serves this child, devoting everything to their progress in this world. Another reason I really like the parent/child model for leadership with horses is the simple fact that horses (confirmed by many animal behavior scientists) have the brain development of a two to four-year-old child. This model helps me keep things in perspective. Before I ever get frustrated, I remember I'm dealing with a young child. I don't ever want to show frustration with a toddler child. As you can imagine or perhaps have experienced, frustration directed at children has devastating and lasting effects.

In reality, however, it is a combination of these last three models that best describes what type of leader we need to be for our horses. Sometimes, as trainers or owners, we're developing an athlete, but we need to remember we're dealing with an animal that didn't choose to be there. We need to be kind, patient, loving, and sometimes firm.

The absolute best way to describe a great relationship between a man or woman and horse is to use the words: **"Leader/Follower."** A leader is someone who cares and realizes that they're dealing with other living, breathing, thinking beings. A leader is someone who wants the best for the follower. He or she serves the follower. The follower does not behave like a robot or machine, but instead expresses love for this kind of leader and in turn wants to please and serve the leader. The leader provides all the physical needs for the follower to survive and even provides emotional needs for the follower to thrive. The leader enriches the life of the follower through serving!

Principle #2: You Get What You Allow

Think of a horse like you think of a toddler child, albeit a very big toddler. If you allow a four-year-old child to speak rudely to other people, he or she will develop a habit of doing so. If you allow that child to eat too much sugar, he or she begins to develop a habit of eating too much sugar. Generally speaking, if you don't allow a certain behavior, it won't occur – or at least not while you're around. *Horses are the same.*

If your horse stands on your toe and you don't do anything about it, he will stand on your toe again. If he barges into your space without any consequences, he'll believe it's totally okay to do it again. Allowing things you don't want to happen encourages those behaviors again.

Now getting into more advanced thinking – if you allow your horse to be "reactive" to scary things by avoiding them or inadvertently rewarding reactive behavior by petting them while they're scared, your horse will continue to be reactive.

I'm *not* suggesting you give out consequences for the horse being reactive, because that will only cause them to be reactive to *you* instead. What I am suggesting is you develop a training program to reduce reactivity in your horse. You'll find this training program available to you right here in this book.

Most horse owners and trainers avoid reactive situations. Instead, good leaders seek out reactive situations in order to work toward changing those situations from reactive to non-reactive.

Here's a simple "don't allow" list:

- Don't allow your horse to be reactive. If you notice reactivity, follow the program in this book.
- Don't allow your horse to mentally shut down or be introverted. If you notice introversion (mental shut down), slowly bring him back to the present moment to be "with you."
- Don't allow your horse to push uninvited into or through your personal space.
- Don't allow your horse to be out of alignment or balance while standing or in motion.
- Don't allow your horse to be distracted or disconnected from you or the task at hand unless it's time for a break.
- Don't allow your horse to be impulsive or lazy.
- Finally, and most importantly: Don't allow yourself to be "frustrated." Frustrated people look like predators!

As you read further into this program you will get many tools to decrease reactivity and increase concentration to illicit more positive responses.

Principle #3: You Are Always Training
Even When You're Not Training

Horses develop habits very quickly. It is widely believed that horses learn faster than us. I'm not certain of this but one thing for sure is they seem to catch on to negative things faster than positive things. If, for instance, you race back to the barn two days in a row, on the third day your horse will do it automatically. If you ask your horse to back up with your reins but fail to release the pressure at the right time, your horse will learn very quickly that your reins don't mean backup.

People often ride their horse like a motorcycle, expecting it to respond to suggestions without hesitation. However, horses are constantly interacting with internal and external pressures; this leaves room for error and misunderstanding simply because they become momentarily distracted. When this happens, it's easy for a novice rider to allow the horse to make repetitive mistakes that ultimately become bad habits.

To put this in perspective, imagine leaving a scary place *before* you felt calm. Imagine leaving that place three times in a row. By the fourth time you would feel fear associated with that place before you even got there and you would avoid that place.

Horses do the same thing. Being clear when riding or teaching your horse is important because *even when you aren't "attempting" to train, you are training.* If you leave a place at the wrong time, if you let go of the reins at the wrong time, if you allow him to stand too close, if you allow her to eat grass while you're trying to communicate, etc. you are still training, and the horse is learning bad habits.

Horses are learning from you all the time. They learn what is allowed and they learn what is not allowed. They learn about your personality. They learn how much you care about them. This is why it's so important to be a good leader.

Principle #4: A Leader Makes No Assumptions Moment by Moment Even After Something is Learned

Day by day, moment-by-moment, emotional beings on this planet shift and change in response to external pressures – and sometimes internal pressures, such as memories or imagined futures.

A poor leader will often make the mistake of assuming that since a horse did something yesterday he can do it again today just as easily. Because horses are emotional beings, this kind of leadership will get you into many frustrating situations with your horse.

Some scientists who study emotion suggest that we tend to shift from emotion to emotion quickly. Usually, we don't experience the same emotions for more than 20 minutes at a time. This means that, at best, every 20 minutes your horse will be a "different" horse, emotionally speaking. Knowing about how emotion changes helps a horseman or horsewoman become a better leader because a good leader doesn't assume the horse that showed up 20 minutes ago (emotionally speaking) will still be around in the next few moments. A good horseman or horsewoman has checks and balances to see if the horse is still connected and relaxed, instead of assuming that connection and relaxation is there, only to find out he/she is mentally spaced out and ready to "explode" under any new pressure. Anything can happen with a horse at any time. Don't assume your horse is perfect and incapable of changing quickly.

Below is a list of things you don't want to assume about you and your horse.

Typical Assumptions People Make

- **"My horse knows this"**

    Horses don't know as much as you think. Even if they can physically do something, that doesn't mean they know *how* to do it, especially if there are any subtle changes in the environment that could change the horse's focus. Even if they know how to do something, they may not know *why* they should do it or why it's more important to perform for you instead of responding to their own ideas.

- **"My horse can't do something"**

It's true; sometimes there are real physical limitations. For instance, an injured horse can't do what a healthy horse can do. However, more often than not, what most people think isn't possible because of some past trauma from negative experience, is in fact possible. It just takes the right timing, the right program, or the right person to help that horse understand something challenging. Just because a horse reacts to certain situations doesn't mean he or she can't (with time and training) overcome those reactions and become a more reliable partner.

- **"My horse won't hurt me"**

Yes, he will, but probably not on purpose. Horses react to lots of different things in life. If you're in the way you could get hurt. He/she might not have been "trying" to hurt you, but you were hurt anyway. Protect yourself by establishing good boundaries and basic safety rules as you venture out into new places. Remember this: "The best horse in the world is still a horse!" Usually a person weighs 20% of what a horse weighs. Mathematically speaking, the odds of you getting hurt are high around horses no matter how "kind" they are. Don't mistake a good horse for a robot. They still have emotions and fears that can come up unexpectedly. Stay alert. Stay safe.

- **"It's me, I must be an idiot"**

Yes, maybe you're not skilled enough to get the task done. Maybe your horse is reacting to your suggestions and feeling confused; but a good leader doesn't let that stop them. They press on (as long as there is no physical danger) because the horse can learn anything in any way given enough time.

Sure, there may be better techniques, and I advocate continuing to look for those; but principally, remember that even the worst technique will work with patience and time, especially if your intent is to support the horse and help that horse thrive in our human world. Don't be so hard on yourself. Stay positive and focused on a plan to help your horse understand you.

- **"The past equals the future"**

I don't care what the past held, except when consoling the person or animal that experienced trauma. What I do care about is what the future holds. The future does not equal the past unless you want it to. Even then it's really hard to exactly recreate the past. Things change. If you use the present moment to start yourself on a journey to positive change you will discover you are capable of that journey. Don't assume that because a horse had an abusive past he can't have a better future and learn to trust people again.

Often people think a horse acts a certain way because of some past trauma, but in fact most of the time it's simply a learned pattern. The horse is doing what he thinks is appropriate for the situation. I try not to get caught up with why the horse is acting up; instead I focus on what I can do to help the horse in the moment, regardless of what happened in the past.

On the other side of this coin is the thought that "just because things are going well today means they will automatically go well tomorrow." This is a massive assumption that can cause great frustration. Take each day as it comes and patiently create the future you want.

- **"There is only one way to do things"**

There are thousands of different ways to do all the different things you want to do with horses. People easily get caught up in a program or technical instruction and find themselves saying, "you can only do things *one* way." This is an assumption. There are literally dozens of ways to train flying lead changes, as well as training circles and lunging on the ground. Dozens of techniques exist for everything. Some techniques work better than others, but usually only in certain situations. Some horses respond differently and require slightly better timing, balance, and strategy from the leader. Stay open to technique and don't throw away what you already know. Sometimes people find a technique doesn't work and then throw it away (never to be seen again) because as a human race we tend to make things universal. We often say, "If it doesn't work now, it never will!" In reality, it may work again in a different situation. Stay open to techniques, but pay closer attention to these principles which will guide you on a path to being a better leader no matter what challenge you face.

Principle #5: True Understanding is Learned Through Practice and Repetition

Repetition is the mother of skill, and just about anything we ask a horse to do is a skill. The more we teach the skill, the better results we get. Often people ask me why their horses don't do certain tasks well. The obvious answer is because they haven't had much time devoted to doing that task. If they say, "But I've been doing it for years," then there is only one other reason why the horse doesn't do that task well. You've been asking in a way that doesn't help the horse understand.

To truly understand something, a horse has to show signs of understanding. Just because a horse does something once or twice does not necessarily mean he/she understands it. The best way to know if your horse understands is if he/she can do it consistently without hesitation. This requires patience and resolve on the part of the trainer.

Complex maneuvers like flying lead changes can take a long time for a horse to understand. A good trainer can get flying lead changes within a few days but that doesn't mean the horse understands it. The proof in the theory is when you put a different rider on and the horse is confused. When this happens, most people blame the rider for not being adequate, but in reality, it's partly the trainer's fault. The trainer assumed the horse understood the maneuver when actually the horse did not. The horse was responding well to the trainer's aids, but didn't actually cognitively understand what he/she was doing, and therefore could not repeat it under different circumstances. Be prepared to take a long time to help a horse not just do something, but truly understand it.

Principle #6: A Leader Makes Training a Positive Experience

Here are two hypothetical stories to illustrate this principle…

Imagine a four-year-old child. You want that child to learn her ABC's and 123's. You decide to start by singing a familiar alphabet song to her, but you notice she isn't participating! You feel emotion welling up inside you. You want her to learn this! You know it's important! So you grab that little girl by the head and force her to look at you. You scream at her and tell her, "This is important!" Out of fear, she responds to you, but not the way you want. She starts to cry! This, in turn, angers you even more and you storm off. In the back of your mind you begin to develop a belief that she has "problems" and can't learn. You hope you can teach her, but if you can't, you'll find someone who will. Also, deep in the back of your mind you feel horrible, like you did something wrong. "I could have handled that better," you'd say. And of course, you are right!

The horse is a sensitive being much like a four-year-old child, highly distractible, playful, and scared. A good trainer knows this and even prepares for this.

Let's take the same story, but now imagine a slightly new and better scenario…

Let's say you begin to teach the ABC's by singing that same song. You recognize she isn't participating. Instead of reacting, you go ahead and finish the song in a playful voice and then softly engage in a conversation.

"Hey there!" you say. "How would you like something sweet to eat?"

"Sure!" she says.

"Okay," you reply. "Follow me! I have something sweet in the cupboard, but you have to sing this silly song all the way to the cupboard to get it. Are you ready? OK???! ABCDEFG..."

Next thing you know, she's singing the ABC song, and within two days she's singing it without the treat. You just did what a good horseman does. You created a positive experience related to a challenging task. Just remember, it's not just what you do but *how* you do what you do that matters!

Reward-oriented training is more powerful than consequence-oriented training. As stated before, techniques are important, but it's better to pay more attention to the way a horse is treated, regardless of technique. If a trainer is consequence-oriented in their style, you'll notice more tension in the horse and more tension in the trainer. This is abusive! You will rarely ever see harmony between horse and human in this situation. However, if a trainer is reward-oriented, you see positive interactions between the horse and human. This is not only beautiful, but it's also more productive.

As a basic rule of thumb or guideline, anytime you have to apply a consequence for a behavior, it has to be balanced with a matching or even exaggerated amount of positive rewards. We've all seen people who are grumpy looking and unsatisfied with everything their horse does. It's not fun to watch and the horse in this situation is not thriving. He's probably just surviving.

On the other side of the coin, we see people who are only positive, reward-oriented in their interactions and they seem to be smiling and happy all the time. These horses tend to thrive. The only balance is when a safety issue comes up such as biting. There must be immediate consequences that match the transgressions. However, promptly following any negative consequences, re-establish some confidence and rapport with the horse to avoid teaching the horse to be reactive.

One quick example: My horse reaches around to bite me in an aggressive manner. I instinctively raise my hand to strike back and drive him away, out of my space! When he leaves, I take a deep breath knowing I just avoided being bitten. Then, within just a few moments, I reach out again to calm the horse, demonstrating that raising my hand does not always mean "go away," but only in safety situations.

Principle #7: Leaders Must Understand Why Things Fail

There are six fundamental reasons horses don't do what we want. Good horsemen and good leaders in any industry can relate to and understand these reasons, therefore avoiding frustrations when things don't go as planned.

Reason 1: Confusion

When things go wrong, a good leader should know that more often than not, someone is confused. Either the horse is confused, or the leader is unclear about their immediate goals. People often mistakenly read poor performance as obstinate behavior. Even when a horse seems to be behaving in an obstinate manner, try to remember that obstinacy is a form of confusion. The horse may know *what* you want but cannot understand *why* it's so important and therefore fail to perform. A good leader plans for confused behavior and helps the horse understand the value of performance through rewards and simple, clear, sequentially progressive goals.

Reason 2: Alignment

One major mistake novice or immature horse trainers make is attempting to accomplish a task to which the horse isn't mentally or physically aligned. Misaligned followers struggle to understand or perform tasks. To illustrate this, think of a furniture mover who's *not* aligned to lift a heavy object and puts himself in a dangerous situation. Alignment is a big topic we'll spend more time on later in the book. For a simple reference to alignment, understand that a horse can't go into a horse trailer it's not looking at or safely carry a rider when he or she is misaligned or out of balance.

Reason 3: Energy

Energy management, as a concept, will be covered in greater detail throughout this book. In basic terms, a horse who has too much energy or too little energy – whether that is physical energy or emotional energy – will struggle to perform certain tasks. Good leaders must learn to manage their horse's energy and find ways to neutralize it.

Reason 4: Concentration or Focus

Distraction is, without any doubt, one of the largest problems horse trainers face. Knowing how to deal with distraction in simple ways, such as re-aligning the horse, will help any leader avoid failing while teaching new and challenging tasks. A good leader must learn to discourage distraction without upsetting or punishing the horse and reward focus every time the horse is trying.

Reason 5: Fear

Fear destroys trust. A good leader must be able to determine if their horse is afraid of something. Perhaps the horse is afraid of the task at hand. Perhaps the horse is afraid of the new elements of his or her environment, or perhaps the horse is afraid of you. Master horsemen can tell the difference and work toward diminishing the fear responses in each situation. Much of this book is dedicated to developing confidence in the horse in all these different circumstances.

Reason 6: Physical Limitation

Horses often fail to perform a simple task (such as cantering) because they feel pain related to the task. Lameness doesn't always show itself in typical ways. Most lameness can be observed when a horse begins to limp or favor one leg. However, many physical limitations aren't so obvious. There are many conditions horses suffer from just like humans. Horses can have sore joints and muscles, bruises, digestion problems, and even brain development problems. Don't assume a horse is being obstinate when he or she isn't doing what you want. Usually he or she is struggling for one of the above six reasons and physical limitations could be one of them. A simple checkup with a local veterinarian can help you find out for sure.

Principle #8: A Leader is Not an "Avoid-aholic"

Being an "avoid-aholic" basically means you habitually avoid things that are hard or uncomfortable. Good horsemen and horsewomen don't do that. Instead, good leaders look for what's not working and creatively find ways to resolve those issues. When things are going well, people have the time of their life with horses. When things aren't going well, people tend to react and then ultimately avoid the situations that caused things to not go so well. I call those situations an "avoid." It's a natural reaction to uncomfortable situations. At my clinics, I invite my students to embrace those challenging situations and train the horse to be more relaxed, more confident, more connected, and more balanced.

When it comes to confidence specifically, I invite my participants to dig for problems. We make a game of it. I say, "Somebody show me something that would cause your horse to react!" At first people are timid. They don't want to upset their horse, so they "walk on eggshells". I invite them to dig a little deeper. "Try to upset your horse!" I say. Of course, they try a little more, but still they act quite timid. Who wants to upset a 1200lb animal anyway, right?

However, it's extremely important (in a safe environment) to set your horse up for random things that could happen in our human world. We need to train our horses to understand what to do in times of crisis. We wrap them in ropes (safely of course) to simulate getting a leg caught in the fence. We flash white flags past their field of vision and past their blind spots to simulate ducks taking off from a pond or large birds elevating from the grass. We bring out noises and flags and plastic bags and tarps, and so many more things to train our horses to be calm under pressure.

When it comes to balance and connection we take a similar approach. We celebrate what's working, but always remember to look for what's not working. We look for imbalances and use our hands and feet to guide the horse to be aligned. We look for distractions that take our horse's attention from us and find ways to cause our horses to re-connect with us. We never assume it's perfect.

A good horseman looks for what's not working in order to resolve problems and help that horse grow. We want to help horses adapt to our human world, to be safe and to thrive. We won't get anywhere by avoiding challenging situations. Of course, we have to set up for safety! So, what we'll do is prepare our environment with safety nets, like working inside a corral instead of out in the field; working with tools that don't cut or tear, such as sharp spurs or bits; working with techniques that give the horse a chance to think through each situation and feel rewarded for being brave. With practice, the horse develops a keen eye for real danger or imagined danger. The horse becomes smarter.

Principle #9: The Leader Enriches the Horse's Life

Every being on the planet needs three things to survive: clean water, good food, and shelter. Without these things, no one can survive. However, a good leader provides more than just what it takes to survive; a good leader provides what it takes to thrive. When it comes to thriving, there are four things to provide for your horse:

1. Positive stimulus to keep from getting too bored. This can come in the form of training programs, obstacles, trail rides, or any positive or playful interaction.

2. Social companionship to keep spirits high. With horses, this usually means giving them another horse to bond and play with, to grow old with.

3. Space to move. Horses need about five to ten acres per horse to move freely at a gallop. Of course, not everyone can provide that much space and therefore must compensate by providing more of the other needs to balance out the horse's need to thrive.

4. Sense of purpose. Most humans and animals derive a sense of purpose through procreation. In other words, the reason for living is to give life to others. Everyone needs to feel valuable and important. Horses are no different. However, helping a horse "feel" like they have a sense of purpose isn't so easy. I've seen horses performing jobs like therapeutic riding for handicap people that absolutely love what they do. You can see they share a real sense of value in the world. But in the exact same arena I've seen other horses fail to feel valuable and hate therapeutic riding. Over time these horses struggle with their purpose because their mind and body deteriorate, whereas when someone loves their job, their mind and body get stronger and they live longer. A good leader and master horse trainer will look for ways to add value to the horse's life through a positive sense of purpose. That could also mean working cattle, riding for children, teaching new riders, pulling a cart, or any form of real value. We, as leaders, have to be careful that just because the job may be valuable to us, it may not be valuable to the horse. Over time, when we see the horse struggling, we must find a new course of action to add a sense of purpose for him or her.

In summary, if one or more of these four needs to thrive are not met or compensated by the leader, the horse will not thrive. The horse will feel like a prisoner instead of a partner. If one or more of the three *survival* needs are not met, the horse, of course, will perish. Good leaders look beyond survival to helping horses fulfill their need to thrive by enriching their life with positive experiences, social structure, space, and a sense of purpose.

To be a good leader takes effort, forethought, and constant observation. When it comes to training programs, good leaders look for the best possible training program to enrich the horse's life, *not enslave it. What you'll find in this book are the tools masters use to enrich a horse's life regardless* of training styles or disciplines. You can use these strategies whether you ride Western, English, Natural, or Traditional. You can use this leadership program if you drive horses or play at liberty on the ground. The steps you'll learn in this book will enhance every aspect of your leadership and communication with your equine partner, no matter what your goals are.

THE FOUR STEP LEADERSHIP FORMULA

Now that our leadership principles are in place as part of our foundation for success in training our horses, it's time to look at the four-step formula we are going to use to accomplish our important goals and increase our leadership with horses.

The formula outlined below *(the 4 B's of leadership)* will be split into sections and each part will be painted in greater detail for you. If you follow these steps in this order, you will not go wrong with your horse. If you step out of order, you may struggle greatly. Once you develop a feel for your horse's needs, you may discover you can bounce back and forth between these four steps. However, in the beginning I always recommend staying close to the sequential order seen below. When I work with young or new horses I always start at step one. When it comes to safety, even with advanced or highly trained horses, setting up and maintaining boundaries is crucial to your success as a leader and trainer.

Step 1: Establishing Clear Boundaries

Every good leader establishes boundaries quickly. In this section, we'll learn how, when, and why.

Step 2: Establishing a True Bond

Friendship is part of leadership. Some disagree, but those who do aren't good leaders. Everyone, including horses, wants to be acknowledged and even loved. In this section, you'll see why it is so important, how to do it, and when to do it.

Step 3: Understanding and Training Bravery

Confidence is a big topic. There are many technical details and I'm going to give you all of what you need to know! You will learn what confidence is and what it looks like in a horse, how it progresses through different stages, where and when to start building confidence, and so much more. Because of its depth and scope, this step is detailed in three separate parts:

- What is confidence?

- What are the strategies to build confidence?

- The 3 goals of confidence training

Step 4: Basic to Advanced Skill development

Only after confidence for your horse has grown will you find he or she is "ready" to learn new things. Many people start with building skills. Don't do that! Build your foundation first. Be the leader your horse deserves. In this shorter section, you will begin to see the value of skill-building and even more details about confidence in a completely new realm: confidence as a learner. As your horse advances through basic skills to advanced skills, you will begin to understand and develop balance and athleticism.

LEADERSHIP STEP 1:

ESTABLISHING CLEAR BOUNDARIES

For safety, it's important to set boundaries with horses. Boundaries keep you alive. You don't want a 1200lb animal stepping on your toes or pulling you around the yard. Assuming you can already catch and halter your horse *(see pitfalls in the back of the book for help with connecting and catching)*, we start setting boundaries on the ground with a halter, a rope, and a driving stick. When the horse learns to respond well to the tools we use and the suggestions we give, he/she will not only be more respectful around us, but in certain, more dangerous situations, you will remember to revert to boundaries to keep your horse focused on you. That will keep both of you safe. Even later, when teaching your horse skills, you'll find he or she will inadvertently step too close or cross over one of your preset boundaries. Remember to focus on retaining your boundary control instead of forcing a task, because when a horse steps out of position, he or she isn't mentally prepared to perform.

THE FIRST BOUNDARY SETUP: BACKUP

Back the horse away from you while you stand in one place. The key is to be the leader. In horse psychology, the one who moves the least is the leader. You can achieve this by driving the horse backward with your ropes or stick. To encourage backward motion, apply pressure by wiggling the rope or driving with your stick in a manner that will cause the horse to respond to you. When your horse responds consistently without hesitation or excessive pressure, you can set up the next boundary. Please refer to the pictures below to illustrate how I do this. *(See pittfals if you have a non-responsive or overreactive horse.)*

Little Shona wiggling the rope to get Legacy to move away.

28

Don shaking the rope to back Sweet T away and out of his space.

THE SECOND BOUNDARY SETUP: FORWARD

Bring your horse back. Simply pulling the rope in to encourage your horse to come back is usually enough support. When your horse hesitates to come back or resists by leaning backward on the halter, you haven't achieved your goal. What we want is for the horse to move without reaction to your suggestions. The first step is to move away. The second is to come back.

If your horse resists, pulls back, or pushes in, these are all signs your horse does *not* have clear boundaries. This is why I always tackle this project first.

Little Shona pulling Legacy back in. One part of boundaries is to ensure the horse responds to the end of the rope.

After pushing Sweet T away, Don invites him back in to make sure he responds smoothly, easily, and equally well, to both backward and forward commands.

Rachel with Dreamy at liberty, bringing him back in after moving him away. In this picture, Rachel is asking for Dreamy to canter toward her. In this case boundaries are well set and Rachel's advancing toward softer and faster responses.

THE THIRD BOUNDARY SETUP: SIDE TO SIDE

Teach your horse to move back and to the left and right. You can achieve this using your same tools. The rope can lead the horse and the stick can drive the horse. This is not much different than lunging or circling. The important thing is to be able to move your horse in four basic directions: backward, forward, left, and right.

Don Driving Sweet T to the side both ways to ensure boundaries are clearly set in all directions. Forward, backward and side-to-side.

Rachel with Pauli asking her to move to the side at liberty. Liberty training is more advanced but the simple principles of boundaries still apply. Teaching a horse to go to the side like this ultimately helps you start training circles or lunging later, and can help balance a horse that leans in too much on the circle.

Boundaries Help with Learning Too:

Boundaries are important for more than just safety. The leader must ensure the horse responds to back, forward, and side-to-side, especially while developing skills like liberty training, circles, preparation for riding, or just about any other task you can imagine. Establishing clear boundaries keeps your horse in a learning frame of mind. Imagine the space between a teacher at the front of the classroom and the students. Maintaining that space is useful to learn new skills and keep the students' (your horse in this case) full attention. Otherwise, the horse can get too close and lose sight of what you're trying to teach.

THE FOURTH BOUNDARY SETUP: STOPPING

Once you can get your horse going to the left or right, you want to be able to stop all motion. This last boundary setup is very important. You must be able to stop your horse in motion and cause him or her to reconnect with you. To do this, simply use the same strategy you used to back him up in the first step. While the horse is in motion to the left or right, simply wiggle the rope until he stops and faces you. Have him or her back up and wait for further instructions. See illustrations for visual support.

Don asking Sweet T to stop in his tracks after moving to the side. When it comes to boundaries, you want the ability to either push away in any direction or bring back from any direction or STOP in any position.

Young man in Brazil learning about boundaries in the Horses for Orphans project.

Side note: Safety and Assertiveness

In some extreme situations (a horse that strikes, kicks, or bites) I have my students do these exercises by standing on something higher or on one side of a fence while the horse is on the other side. Learning that you are a leader before you are a friend is important to your horse. Otherwise, when the horse feels scared or irritated in any way, he'll run right over the top of you or else pull away from you. However, if he sees you as a leader, he'll look to you for information instead of reacting to you. He'll stay in a learning frame of mine. If you practice establishing these boundaries for your horse he'll remember how to respond to you in high-pressure situations and respect your personal space.

The key is that we want our horses to look at and line up with us, physically. We want them to learn to face us and stand away from us. We want them to learn to move to the left and to the right and face up again without any resistance. The whole point is that in any kind of emergency you can instantly get your horse's attention and keep them in a safe position relative to you.

To be clear, you know when your boundaries are set up well with your horse because your horse stops pulling back on the rope, stops pushing into your space, stops pushing side to side to avoid focusing on you. Put simply, well-established boundaries means your horse responds well enough to you at any time to stand still at a safe distance.

As you advance to the next steps you'll discover times when your horse steps over the boundaries. They either pull back on the rope or push into your space or escape to the left or right to avoid focusing on you. When this happens, remember to reset the boundaries. Go back to step one, even if you're in the middle of teaching a new task or skill. And be as assertive as necessary to remind your horse of your boundary lines. Maintaining your boundaries keeps you safe and your horse in a learning frame of mind.

Ingela establishing better leadership and positioning herself in a safer place by standing on something high. Anytime you have a horse that is likely to bite, kick or charge, it's useful to position yourself on top of or behind something like a fence while you establish boundaries. At least until your horse becomes predictably responsive to you.

How do Boundaries apply to riding?

Masterful trainers almost always start on the ground. Doing so, will develop a horse's thought and behavior patterns long before riding becomes part of what you do. However, once a trainer does begin riding, it doesn't mean the horse will be "perfect". Good riders often find themselves resetting boundaries even while in the saddle.

What that means is when you ask a horse to stand still, and he moves anyway, he is overstepping boundaries and it should be addressed as such. There is no need to be mean or mad about it, just clear, calm, and direct. When a horse is walking, but speeds up beyond your desired speed or slows down, or steps off your desired line of travel to the side, these too are boundary issues and can be addressed as such. By simply asking your horse to reset his or her position and re-align with the direction you're going, you can help a horse focus and stay safe.

In the picture to the left, Don had to reset Monty's position many times before Monty would allow him to stand without walking off.

Only after the horse is responsive enough to listen to your suggestions about boundaries, is it truly safe to go to the next step… Bonding!

LEADERSHIP STEP 2:

ESTABLISHING A TRUE BOND

Once *Leadership Step 1: Establishing Clear Boundaries* is firmly established – I mean so well established that you can easily move your horse around and away from you without resistance – then Step 2 is all about creating a bond. Bonding with your horse is important. I've seen horses that are very respectful of boundaries but "hate" people. They don't feel any love or friendship, because that person never shows any real value toward the horse.

Rachel and Dreamy

Douglas with his horse in the Horses for Orphans project.

On the flip side, I've seen people bond with their horses before establishing boundaries. These horses tend to "love" people, but in any kind of emergency they run right over them. Horses can weigh upwards of 1000 to 2000lbs depending on their breed, and all it takes is one wrong step to break a person's body. Horrific accidents happen every day in the world of horses because boundaries were not clearly established in a safe way, and if the rider proceeds to train skills or try to build a friendship without clear boundaries, disastrous outcomes may occur. As important as bonding is in our relationship with horses, **boundaries almost always take precedence over bonding**. The only exception to this rule is when a horse can't be caught. In this special case, a small amount of bonding may have to take place just to make a physical connection with the horse.

On that same note, if too much bonding takes place before boundaries, another problem can arise. Let me give you an example. I've seen people bond before setting up boundaries and never really make it to Step 3 – Bravery Training – because that horse simply won't put up with anything they don't feel comfortable with. It would be like building a pattern of "the easy life" full of love and kindness and then one day introducing something hard. Your horse would resist the hard things and cause you to start avoiding anything challenging.

The important thing to remember is that boundaries clearly come first. Once they are established, bonding must also take place. Without bonding you will not have a great relationship, and you will not achieve great things together. Horses are sensitive to what you are thinking and feeling. They can tell when you care about them or when you only care about your own goals that you impose upon them.

The best horsemen in the world all agree: "Horses don't care how much you know if you don't show how much you care!" Without bonding, your horse's relationship with you feels like a slave to the master.

Bonding is extremely important and it's one of the easiest and most rewarding things to do with horses. It takes very little effort and horses love you for it. **All you have to do is think about what horses like most... and give it to them.** Horses love being massaged, scratched, brushed, and groomed. They usually have favorite spots on their body where they *can't* personally scratch very well and you can be the best friend in the world by indulging in their desire to have that spot attended to. They also love treats.

Horses love treats; Rachel is giving Pauli a treat for her effort.

Safety note on treats

I use treats for some circumstances, such as teaching a horse to enjoy being caught or enjoy putting in effort for a task but I don't "over treat" my horse because treats tend to excite the emotions rather than relax the horse. When it comes to training a horse to be confident we don't want excitement. I've seen horses enjoy a treat and then suddenly become a "cookie monster" and forget their boundaries. If you can easily remind them of their boundaries, you can use treats as a bonding tool.

Special Note

Some horses don't show signs of appreciation at first when it comes to bonding. These horses are very skeptical by nature and may have been mistreated by humans in the past. The point is that you break through this problem by spending more bonding time than usual. You want to see your horse show signs of appreciation before you jump to Step 3 (Bravery) in this formula, even if it takes days.

One particular colleague of mine named Andy, decided to purchase a zorse (half zebra, half horse). This zorse, named Stormy, would use her natural born talent to out-maneuver my colleague and quickly pull the rope from Andy's hands. Once free, she would run as far away as she could; it

didn't matter what direction. After several such instances, my friend finally realized he was missing an important part of the picture with his equine partner. **They had no bond.**

Andy made a point to create the bond, but his little zorse showed no interest. After days went by and little progress to show, he finally decided to take things to a new level. He pulled out his sleeping bag and pillow, night light, snacks, and camped right next to his four-legged friend who stood just inches away in another stall. Days went by! Then something magical happened. Stormy approached him, touched him, and nuzzled against him. The bond was created. Together, they became one of the most inspirational duos of their time. Anyone who has seen them would concur, there was something more than training going on there: something almost spiritual.

It's important your horse knows you care before you start training other skills; otherwise you're no different in their eyes than the last person who treated them like an all-terrain vehicle with no feelings – like a slave! Try to think more like my friend with the zorse and find a way to show you appreciate your equine partner.

Take some time to look at your own horse now. How do you know your horse appreciates your partnership? Are you willing to discover what he/she loves most and show that you care? Are you willing to be the leader he/she always hoped for?

Andy Booth and his striped partner, Stormy the zorse. Stormy is now retired and living in France.

Ingela bonding with her horse.

Don knows what Legacy wants: scratching! Bonding is about giving them what they love most.

Pauli enjoying a scratch in the flank area.

How will you know your horse appreciates your bonding time? Your horse will show you the visible signs of enjoyment or relaxation! They show it in their eyes and in their face; they literally show signs of tension disappearing or signs of enjoyment by twisting their head and stretching out while being scratched. Sometimes they even show you where they want to be scratched, or you'll see them lower their body posture and breathe slower as you massage. They behave much the same way we do when we are enjoying a scratch or when we are feeling relaxed.

Any sign of tension means our bond still needs some work. If the tail is clamped tight or the breathing is fast and short or the neck-set is high or the lips are pierced closed, you know you haven't got to the place where your horse trusts you or likes you. Keep going. Then later, after you've done parts of Steps 3 and 4 in the formula, come back and reestablish the bond.

Keep in mind that a bond is for a lifetime. It's not something you do every once in a while. It's something you do whenever you can, especially if you're training your horse to do difficult tasks. It's easy for the horse to think you don't care and begin to believe you're just a slave driver!

You want them to remember you do care and you are a friend too. Come back to your bonding. Use it consistently to show you care and also use it as a reward every time your horse does something well.

Be careful not to use bonding when your horse is scared because that's when bonding has a negative effect. I see people trying to bond with a scared horse and inadvertently reward the fearful tendency. Guide your horse to be brave and respect boundaries, then reward the horse. Don't reward a reactive horse by petting and soothing in the same way you would bond. Usually with a reactive horse you have to be the leader. Reestablish the boundaries and then bond once he's back on your page.

Leisure time is valuable time.

Taking the time to care can make all the difference as a leader. Like Weverson in the picture above, bonding with his horse during rest time.

A true bond means true trust. This horse obviously "likes" Douglas.

Ingela showing affection and the horse responding with obvious appreciation.

Don bonding with Sweet T in the early stages. Looking for what he likes most. Is it scratching around eyes, ears, or anywhere else on his body?

Ingela taking a moment to reinforce the bond during training.

Rachel and Dreamy expressing a true bond.

The value of a true bond goes beyond just friendship. The bond is an integral part of leadership. Without it, you will *not* succeed in influencing your horse in a positive way.

Bonding also goes well beyond ground work. Bonding should be something you do often, even when riding. Simply resting, reaching up to scratch behind the ears, or showering your horse with praise, love, and treats of any kind can all be done while riding. Infuse bonding into your regular training by returning to give your horse what he or she loves, as a reward for giving you everything you love.

Rachel and Pauli bonding while riding.

LEADERSHIP STEP 3:

BRAVERY - UNDERSTANDING AND TRAINING CONFIDENCE

We've made it to the heart of the book now! In this section, we're going to find out what confidence really is, and then demonstrate seven distinct strategies for training confidence. Then *finally address the three basic goals of confidence training:*

Contents of this section include:

4 stages of confidence (not tolerate, tolerate, tolerate/relax, total relaxation)

3 types of stimulus horses react to (tactile, auditory, visual)

7 confidence-building strategies (approach and retreat, flash training and more)

3 goals every trainer should have when building confidence (stand still, motion, obstacles)

UNDERSTANDING CONFIDENCE

What is confidence? Confidence is defined by Webster as "firm trust". Although this definition is congruent with what we want to establish, it doesn't quite capture all the details necessary to clearly define the progression of confidence. I believe a good trainer is interested in measuring progress. Trust is something gradually attained.

Below is an illustration of the natural progression of confidence.

The Four Stages of Confidence and Trust

Stage 1 is what we call "CANNOT TOLERATE"

This means that your horse cannot tolerate what is happening and feels as though he or she *must* move or escape. Repetition and practice help you advance beyond Stage 1. A horse that cannot tolerate stimulus is also quite dangerous to be close to. Hence, clearly reinforcing your boundaries and personal space can help you get through this delicate time. Never be afraid to keep yourself and your horse safe, even if it means abandoning the very things you're trying to do, in order to re-set your leadership status.

Young horse in Stage 1 of bravery training. Does NOT tolerate saddle.

Sweet T in Stage 1 of bravery (or) confidence training. Does NOT tolerate the flag.

Stage 1: Sweet T NOT tolerating the umbrella.

Stage 2 is what we call "TOLERATE"

This means that a horse *can* stand still while "crazy" things are going on around him or her. It doesn't mean he's totally relaxed; it means he's respectful enough and trusting enough to tolerate what's happening around him.

Stage 2: Just tolerating, but not accepting or relaxing.

Don with Sweet T and the umbrella and stock whip showing moving past Stage 1 into Stage 2: Tolerating.

Notice the raised head indicating we have not achieved total relaxation yet.

Stage 3 is what we call the "TOLERATE/RELAX" stage.

Stage 3 is an in-between place where you see signs of letting go emotionally. Just like in the bonding stage you'll see visible signs of the breathing slowing, or the tension in the muscles relaxing. The eyes begin to soften. He may even cock a leg and stand on three legs instead of four. His neck and jaw will begin to lower and soften. But in this stage, he won't stay relaxed. He'll often pop back and forth between a tense posture and a relaxed posture because he's still a little unsure. A good trainer can get to this stage in as little as 20 minutes, but it can also take that same trainer 20 days to get to this stage with a more difficult horse.

Pauli is starting to relax a little around the kids. Stage 3: not total or consistent relaxation, but certainly better than Stage 2 or Stage 1.

Stage 3: You can see Sweet T is tolerating and showing signs of relaxation, but isn't totally trusting. There is noticeable softness in the expression with more signs of relaxation, but this relaxed expression is inconsistent, indicating Stage 4: total relaxation is still yet to come.

Training isn't over until he gets to Stage 4, even if his training is spread out over days, weeks, months, or even years.

Stage 4 is what we call "TOTAL RELAXATION"

Stage 4 is a noticeable difference in the horse's attitude toward the stimulus. You don't see any signs of tension or reactivity at this stage. You see a calm horse that's not afraid of anything and it stays that way consistently day-by-day, moment-by-moment. It's rare to get to this stage in one session, but over a matter of days and weeks a horse can develop this kind of trust with the person and all the "crazy" stimulants we subject them to.

Stage 4: Total relaxation.

Douglas (above) Fabricio (below) from the Horses for Orphans projects showing totally relaxed horses.

SPECIAL NOTE – HOW TO TEST FOR TOTAL RELAXATION

Sometimes people misread the horse as being at stage four (total relaxation) when really, they are introverted (shut down mentally); they've checked out. They look calm, but they're bubbling with emotion on the inside.

You can easily check for introversion or what I sometimes call "frozen body language" by simply asking the horse to move any part of his/her body. How he reacts tells a lot about how he's feeling.

Checking the tail to see if the horse is holding tension (a loose tail is a good sign)

For instance: If he resists a simple request to move a body part (such as lifting the tail, dropping the head, or moving the feet), he's probably mentally shut down. If he reacts negatively, it means he was *definitely* shut down. If he explodes, it means he was extremely introverted. But… if he simply yields to the pressure without resistance or hesitation… this means he's relaxed and calm and mentally awake to what's going on.

Also, sometimes the horse seems okay in one area, but is not completely relaxed in every circumstance. For example, your horse may have confidence with one particular obstacle, but when that obstacle approaches the horse from a different angle or with different random timing or energy, it can still cause a reaction. Therefore, it's useful to work with a horse from all angles.

In Review So Far:

Total confidence is when the horse can handle any obstacle coming from any direction at any speed at any time. When we begin to work through the types of stimulus that bother horses, keep in mind we want to train them to handle those types of stimulus from any direction, speed, or random timing.

Below: Stage 4 (Total Relaxation from all positions)

SIDE NOTE:

THE CHALLENGE OF TEACHING CONFIDENCE

Why is it so hard to teach confidence? Horses are prey animals, whereas humans are natural predators. Horses have an instinct stronger than mental reasoning. They have millions of years of genetic coding telling them to fight or flee under pressure. Horses find it hard to think clearly under any kind of pressure. Humans also struggle to think clearly under pressure, but horses are even more sensitive to danger than most people, and what might seem like nothing to us, might put the fear of death in a horse. They easily believe they could get hurt or even be killed with new circumstances and stimuli.

So, remember to be a patient leader while your horse learns to trust you and new challenges. Each new challenge can take more time than you might expect, so don't get discouraged when training takes longer than you hoped.

Also, avoid using techniques that could endanger your horse, such as "hard tying" or "running hobbles" that leave the horse with no opportunity to escape. Any technique that enslaves the horse's mind and body should be avoided. The only "fair" thing to do is work *with* their mind in a way that encourages conscious choice. Decades ago it was common place to use such horrific methods as tying horses down and hobbling feet as a means of forcing compliance. Fortunately, many of those techniques have been outlawed; but some trainers still insist on imposing confidence or "breaking" the horse. Which really means breaking the horse's will and spirit.

Instead, be the leader that cares enough to take the longer, safer road that leads to happier, healthier horse/human partnerships.

THREE STIMULI THAT AFFECT A HORSE

So what are horses bothered by? Horses react to three types of stimulus: tactile (touching), auditory (noises), and visual. Our goal is to get your horse to stop reacting to all three.

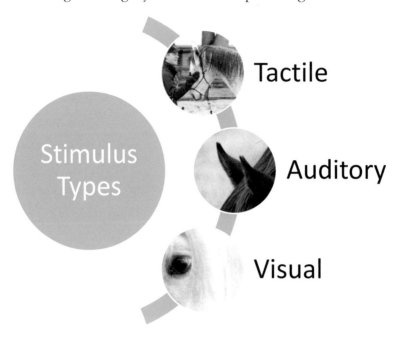

TACTILE STIMULUS

Tactile stimulus means anything that bumps, pokes, prods, jabs, rubs, slaps, taps, massages, squeezes, etc. In my seminars, I have people test with their hands (or in some cases a long stick for safety) all the typical spots that horses don't want to be touched, such as outside and inside their mouth, their ears, eyes, nostrils, belly, flank, private parts, inside of the leg muscles, under the tail, and the bottom side of their feet.

Once a horse can be touched in all those areas we start adding in bumps and pokes, prods and taps in varying degrees of intensity. We take ropes to squeeze around their belly and flank. We do everything and anything we can imagine to "desensitize" our horse to random things that happen in our human world. I invite my students to "dig deep" into the reactivity of their horses. I invite them to not "walk on eggshells" around their horses. I want them to find what triggers fear responses in their horses and creatively find ways to resolve the fear issues.

I have a saying I want you to remember:

"A good horseman is always looking for tension and creatively finding ways to take it out!"

Bonding every time you get a good change in your horse is a good strategy for training trust and rewarding the horse for losing the tension. Strategically, however, there is more you need to know to be good leader. There are specific techniques we'll go over soon.

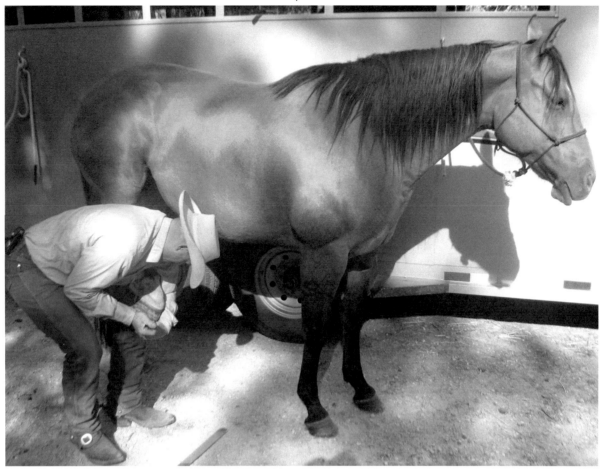

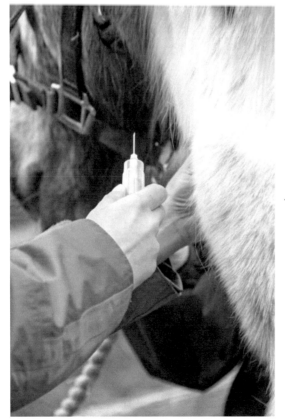

Above: Ben touching/holding his horse's feet. Testing her confidence with tactile stimuli in different areas.

The needle is the ultimate tactile experience. Starting with a toothpick or fingernail is a better and safer method to prepare for needles.

Don carefully exposing a young mare to the tactile sensation of ropes in odd places; carefully, being the optimal word because, done incorrectly, or with poor feel and timing, this technique could go wrong quickly and cause more harm than good. By the way, can you guess which stage of tolerance she is working through in the picture?

SIDE NOTE:

Ropes hold extraordinary value as a master horseman or horsewoman *(not just for cowboys)* because with ropes, the trainer can stay safe while teaching a horse not to react to getting caught in a fence or tightening the girth strap on a saddle. Horses that can respond without reacting to the tightening of ropes around his body or legs are typically safer horses.

AUDITORY STIMULUS

Auditory stimulus is usually the next port of call. Once a horse can handle bumps and taps, slaps and rubs, squeezes and pokes, or the feeling of ropes dragging and holding on the legs or body, it's time to start teaching them to handle noises. I want my horse to be non-reactive to whips, bangs, and slaps. I want my horse to be fearless when a plastic bag crinkles or a tarp rustles. I want my horse to stand still while a gun is fired or a noisy truck drives past with flapping tarps. I want my horse to look for my expression and trust all will be okay when they hear chainsaws cutting trees, nail guns and skill saws hacking away at new building sites, and every other noise you can imagine. I want my horse, and ultimately your horse, to be "bombproof."

Naturally, we must start with more basic ideas than firing a 45-caliber gun, but those who hope to have a completely confident horse will eventually tackle bigger projects like mounted shooting.

Ingela with a horse who's never seen a large group of children and a group of children who've never seen a horse, all part of the Horses for Orphans projects. This horse must learn to tolerate and accept the new noises.

Top: Ingela riding near noisy machinery.

Bottom Left: Don training Monty to accept the stock whip for auditory stimulus while riding.

Below: Renee demonstrating confidence and control while shooting her 45-caliber pistol from her horse. Mounted shooting is one of the toughest auditory experiences a horse can learn to handle because of the extremity of the noise, added visual sensation of flashing fire and the smell of burning powder.

All new skills, including auditory desensitization, should start on the ground. Above, Don is helping Sweet T accept the stock whip for the first time. Can you guess which stage of tolerance Sweet T is showing?

1. Not tolerate?   2. Tolerate?   3. Tolerate/Relax?   4. Total Relaxation?

VISUAL STIMULUS

Visual stimulus is what we address last because sometimes a horse can't handle a scary thing it sees. Sometimes, scary things come uninvited into the environment we're sharing. First, I'll address "the elephant in the room" by resolving the biggest problem that is presently happening, then move to address other things. Usually, however, with a more connected horse, I address visual things last because visual stimulus tends to create the most reactivity and I want my students and horses to be well set up before they get into these types of complex situations.

Visual stimulants come in all sorts of shapes and sizes. I want my horse to be able to handle tarps, flags, bags, waving hands, balloons, saddles, ropes dragging and swinging, other horses trotting by, trucks, cars, garbage cans, mailboxes, water, jumps, trailers (outside and inside), dogs, kids, fast approaches, slow approaches, wheel chairs, motorcycles, buggies, other animals, trampolines, people working on a roof, tractors, trees being cut down. You name it...I want my horse to handle it! I want my horse to be confident I have things under control. I want my horse to be confident the world isn't ending.

I start with easy things and advance quickly. I am constantly looking for what bothers my horse and finding ways to take the reactivity away and create a positive experience. Remember principle number seven, don't be an avoid-aholic. When you see a challenge, take it on.

Total confidence with visual stimulus.

Stage 4: Total confidence with a tarp while standing still.

Christina and Maeve demonstrating confidence with visual stimulus.

Christina and Maeve demonstrating total confidence with visual, auditory, and tactile stimuli.

Ingela showing visual stimulus does not have to be scary.

SPECIAL NOTE

My goal is to get my horse to be completely non-reactive to stimulus but if I can't achieve that, then as a minimum requirement, I want the ability to tell my horse to pay attention to me instead of that crazy thing out there. This is simple to accomplish. Just remember your boundary games (Step 1) and re-establish your boundaries anytime your horse reacts to the environment. By doing boundary games you'll actually train more self-confidence in the horse and you'll begin to believe you can manage more complex situations.

LAST NOTE ON "WHAT IS CONFIDENCE?"

Confidence Must be Learned in Different Positions

We've talked about what it looks like. We've talked about what types of things horses are bothered by. But we haven't talked about confidence in different positions around the horse. Just because I can stand in front of my horse with an umbrella doesn't mean I can stand to the side, behind, or on top of my horse with an umbrella. All these different positions should be addressed with tactile, auditory, and visual stimuli as time goes by. See all the different positions on the next page. As time goes by, working toward building your horse's confidence from all directions will help create that "perfect", or at least "almost perfect", safe horse. I say, "almost perfect" because a horse is still a horse or course.

Notice all the different positions:
In front, at the sides, at hips, behind, on top, and underneath.

SEVEN CONFIDENCE-BUILDING STRATEGIES

Before I send you out to build confidence (to create that "bombproof horse") we need to set up some strategy for training confidence. We know what confidence looks like, we know the different things that trigger fear or tension or reactivity, we know that horses have a hard time learning to be confident, and we know it takes time to train. What we need to know next are specific strategies and when to use those specific strategies.

There are seven basic strategies for helping a horse become more confident. We've addressed the specifics of what we want them to be confident about. Now it's time to make sure you have some feel and some tactical advantage when you're dealing with the real thing. The following strategies require a little feel, timing, and intuition:

1. **Reset Boundaries and Realign the Horse**
2. **Approach and Retreat**
3. **Move Closer, Stay longer**
4. **Flooding**
5. **Flash Training**
6. **Allow and Encourage Curiosity**
7. **Combinations**

With practice and experience, your intuition to choose your strategies, will grow.

STRATEGY NUMBER 1: RESET BOUNDARIES AND REALIGN THE HORSE

This strategy is the simplest and sometimes most effective of all the strategies. When a horse is scared, one basic thing you can do is ask the horse to stop, move back to where he started (physically), and start over. This means that whatever you were doing before is not as important as getting back to the starting point. This little break away from the intense focus of training confidence, yet still demanding attention and respect, is usually a nice reprieve from the pressure the horse may be feeling. After several "re-sets" as I call them, your horse may just start to tolerate that scary thing.

One particular horse I played with could not stand to be poked by a needle. The only strategy I employed was to move him back to his starting point every time he moved away from the needle that was approaching him or away from me in general.

This strategy does take some time to make a difference, yet it's easy to remember and effective in some situations to cause a really big change in your horse's confidence and trust that you won't hurt him.

All he has to do is keep still. By the way, you can't – or at least shouldn't – attempt to hold your horse within small boundaries with sheer force. That is extremely dangerous. You're better off to teach them to stand still by simply moving them back very quickly to the position every time they choose to move. This way they have the choice to stand still or move, but ultimately be moved back to the position. This is an effort to make the wrong thing difficult and the right thing easy. Make the position you want comfortable and all other positions uncomfortable.

After a while, every horse in the world chooses to stand still. That doesn't mean they are relaxed; it just means they trust enough to tolerate what's going on. Further training will be necessary.

STRATEGY NUMBER 2: APPROACH AND RETREAT

This strategy is as simple as it sounds. Let me give an example. Let's say I'm training my horse to handle a tactile sensation; rubbing his ears for instance. At first, he can't stand it, so I simply rub *near* his ear then take my hand away to a more neutral place, perhaps closer to his nose. Then I try again, each time moving closer to the ear, then retreating to a neutral place. Back and forth I go until finally he accepts me touching his ears. If I reward him for allowing me to touch him, he'll quickly realize that being touched there isn't so bad and maybe it's even good.

Every challenge, even visual and auditory challenges, can be met with this strategy. Approach and retreat is simple, effective, and easy to remember. Even if you had no other ideas on what to do to solve your horse's fear, you would succeed with this strategy. It's not the only "trick" you want in your bag, but it's one of the best.

STRATEGY NUMBER 3: MOVE CLOSER, STAY LONGER

This strategy is much the same as the approach and retreat, but the timing is different. Instead of approaching and moving away, you approach, hold steady at any particular threshold, then retreat when you see signs of tension dissipating. Remember, a threshold is what we call that place or time when you notice your horse's tension raise in order to prepare for fighting or fleeing. When training confidence, you must become aware of "fear thresholds" in order to be more effective as a leader.

STRATEGY NUMBER 4: FLOODING

Safety Note: This strategy is more complicated, but can be very effective. Let me be clear: a person can completely ruin a horse's confidence by using this technique incorrectly. However, done correctly, a good trainer can make an immediate and lasting change. I always advise caution with this technique, but that doesn't mean you shouldn't learn how and when to use it.

Here is an example of flooding: You approach, approach, approach, approach, literally "flooding" the horse's emotional system. Sometimes a horse just won't make the breakthrough with approach and retreat techniques. Occasionally they need that extra something. In these special cases, I will hold the pressure up close to the horse for long periods of time until the horse realizes it's not going away. When I see that positive shift, I'm looking for, such as holding still, I back away.

Example: Recently a thoroughbred mare, just rejected from the track (obviously mistreated and malnourished), would not let me near her ears to touch her with my hand. She had a halter on, so somehow someone got it over her neck and ears, but there was still an obvious and even dangerous issue with her ears. She would strike or even bite if she felt you were going to touch her ears. After some time of using the first two strategies I finally decided to apply the flooding strategy.

Naturally, I set myself up for success by using a long stick instead of my hand. That way, I was out of reach if she tried to strike at me or bite me. Many spectators standing nearby asked me if she was a "mean" horse. I simply replied, "No, she wasn't being mean. She just has no other options in her mind when she feels threatened." She was scared and reacting in a mean way to preserve her life.

I reached for her ears with the stick. It had a soft padded end so I couldn't jab her eyes or ears. She did her thing and I did mine. I physically rubbed her ears as she struck out and tried to bite, and sometimes all at once; but I didn't let off. I kept coming at her ears, strategically switching from left to right every time she drifted too far in one direction. I also flooded tactile and visual stimulus in every other area of her neck, legs, feet, nose, and midsection. "Flooding" is what it sounds like. Imagine being washed over or flooded with stimulus until you just don't care that you're soaking wet anymore.

Side Note: Again, I reiterate: Flooding is dangerous for both you and your horse. If done wrong, things can go badly! If you do decide to try flooding, do it in slow motion and add in more retreating and less approaching. Don't get yourself or your horse injured by pushing too hard or too fast. Don't do it in an area that you could get trapped, don't do it in an area where your horse could fall and become injured, and don't do it with tools that are ineffective at guiding the horse to a better solution (such as ropes that are too short).

To finish the story with the rejected and mistreated mare… Within minutes, she quickly realized she was not going to get out of this one by reacting to the stimulus as she had obviously done many times before. She had to think of some other option. She'd tried pushing into me, kicking me, striking me, biting me, bolting, rearing, and pulling back. Nothing had worked. The stimulus never quit until she realized she was out of options. Finally, I had her "thinking" instead of reacting. When her options were exhausted, she decided to stand quietly – still tense, but quiet. Once I had her doing that, I softened my approach and reverted to more of an approach and retreat format until she allowed me to touch her ears… even with my hand. Now fast forward. Today this same mare is confidently accepting all human inputs and even competing without ever struggling to put on her bridle.

STRATEGY NUMBER 5: FLASH TRAINING

Flash training is a technique I use to help a horse handle sudden, random stimulus. Imagine walking your horse around the corner of the house when suddenly your neighbor opens the door and your horse spooks, jumps on your foot, and sends you to the hospital with broken toes.

Your horse isn't afraid of your neighbor or doors opening, in general. Your horse is afraid of something randomly flashing in his field of vision. To help a horse develop confidence in relation to flashing objects or anything that happens suddenly, I often use the flash training strategy.

Flash training is a simple simulation of what scares the horse. I re-create the possible scenarios in which my horse may react to sudden stimuli. Then I work randomly in varying degrees of intensity with that stimulus or simulated stimulus. All the while keeping track, my horse respects my boundaries.

Only after boundaries are clearly set up would I ever attempt to experiment with flash training. I begin by helping a horse handle flashing visual objects (such as flags or plastic bags), then move onto sudden tactile and auditory sensations. I'm repetitive enough to make a difference in the horse's memory. So after a short while, the horse starts to realize that when things *happen suddenly* they don't have to be afraid anymore.

STRATEGY NUMBER 6: ALLOW AND ENCOURAGE CURIOSITY

When a horse pokes his nose out in front of his body to reach for and smell an object, allow it. Too many trainers focus on getting a task done and missing the special moments of confidence-building that come quite naturally through curiosity. When a horse is curious he or she is trying to understand something. Curiosity builds confidence and all great horse trainers use curiosity as part of their training repertoire.

For instance, if a horse leans forward into a horse trailer for the first time, don't push. Wait! When a horse leans forward over a jump for the first time or into a river for the first time, don't push. Wait! Allow his curiosity to push himself over. Allow him time to engage with the object that bothers him. Encourage him to understand what you want, not just be subjected to it. I often allow my horse to smell my saddle, my clothes, my stock whip, or tarp, or plastic bag on the end of a stick. I encourage and even reward my horse for smelling the horse trailer or pawing at the water for the first time. All these behaviors indicate the horse is processing and needs a bit more time. There is no need to push harder and no need to speed up the process.

STRATEGY NUMBER 7: COMBINATIONS

Just as it sounds, this is a strategy that involves all other strategies. As an expert, I need the flexibility to adjust to any situation. Combining strategies gives me the most options.

For example, I can move slowly toward a particular goal with approach and retreat strategies. Then, if the horse is not making positive changes, I can change things up, using "flooding" or "move closer, stay longer" techniques. Finally, I can introduce flash training to simulate reactions under sudden pressure. If I need, I can slow down again, allow my horse to smell or otherwise engage in the challenge. Using my judgment and intuition, I can become very effective at training my horse's confidence.

Most horses would react to random, challenging stimuli or experiences. However, after you do sufficient bravery training with your horse, you will find you have a happier, more agreeable partner.

USING YOUR INTUITION AND READING YOUR HORSE

There are of course varying degrees of intensity and speed at which one can use the above strategies. These are not rules. You still must think your way through and feel your way through the process.

Use your intuition. Read the horse. See how he or she reacts. If he pushes through a boundary, re-establish it! If he seems like he might soften, slow down and use more approach and retreat. If you see he is doing well but you're unsure he's really, truly relaxed, stimulate with flash training. If you feel he just isn't letting go and it's not going to resolve by using approach and retreat, try flooding. Apply the kind of intensity and speed you think will be appropriate and adjust as you go along. Make no assumptions that "robotic" training methods will work. Be creative and have fun, but always keep your safety and your horse's safety at the front of your mind.

One last thought: Like a four-year-old child, horses need breaks when learning to be confident. Remember, "Rome wasn't built in one day!" Take your time and be safe. Keep your boundaries clear and your bond strong. Most confidence issues can be resolved with these strategies alone.

Don with Monty taking his time to process the next best step.

THE 3 GOALS OF CONFIDENCE TRAINING

1. Goal 1 is teaching a horse to stand still while scary things happen around him/her.

2. Goal 2 is teaching your horse to be non-reactive while in motion as scary things happen.

3. Goal 3 is teaching your horse to cross scary thresholds (that moment of hesitation when a horse is asked to move out of their comfort zone, such as a water crossing).

CONFIDENCE BUILDING GOAL 1: STANDING STILL

Using our firm grasp of what confidence looks like and how to gain trust, it's now time to start practicing. We'll start by teaching the horse to stand still while things happen around him.

Strategically, it's simple. With our bond set in stone and our boundaries clearly drawn, we conclude that our horse is completely focused on us. In my seminars, I ask my participants to prove the bond and boundaries are clearly set. When they do, they also prove total concentration from the horse. With a horse totally focused on you, you can start to stimulate him. You can start digging for things he doesn't like. You've already spent time finding out what he does like in the bonding step. Now let's find out what he doesn't like.

In this step, you are actually going to attempt to "spook" your horse. What I mean is to simulate a real life experience the horse might have. To be clear, I don't want your horse to spook in the end... I just want to simulate a spook to teach a new way to respond when spooky or scary things happen. Naturally you would start on the ground and advance to riding.

The trick is... you can only take the spook out of him by finding out what spooks him. Once you find what bothers your horse most, tackle that problem. Don't be an avoid-aholic! Using the strategies of approach and retreat and other variations of the things we talked about earlier, you'll be able to convince your horse to tolerate things and then eventually relax with those things going on around him.

The end goal of confidence building or bravery training is to teach your horse to stand still and remain relaxed under extreme pressures, including getting up and riding.

Dreamy is confident and relaxed enough for just about anything!

Look at the horse lying down. Total confidence!

Relaxed and bonding in a position that would otherwise make any other horse nervous!

Confidence to fish from the back of your horse… now that's living!

Teaching a horse to stand still while things happen around or on top of him can be tricky to accomplish, but ultimately, it is one of our grandest goals. Review the strategies for teaching confidence, including resetting boundaries and re-aligning the horse. When the horse moves, move him back into place and start over. Before long you will be doing just about anything you can imagine with a confident horse! Remember to be progressive to the point where one day your horse doesn't just tolerate stimulus but also remains totally relaxed in the presence of pressure.

Once you can do things while standing still, it's time to tackle the next goal: confidence in motion!

CONFIDENCE BUILDING GOAL 2: CONFIDENCE IN MOTION

We've talked a lot about getting a horse confident to stand for something, but we also need to address their confidence when it comes to seeing those scary things while they are in motion.

The same basic strategies apply. For instance, if I want my horse to accept a rope swinging or perhaps dragging on the ground next to him while he's walking along, I'll use a simple approach and retreat technique. I'll begin by adding more rope, then less rope, adding small swings, then bigger swings. With lots of rewards and rest time your horse will realize that ropes in motion mean the same thing as ropes while standing.

The tricky part about training horses to accept things while they're moving their feet is to get them to keep moving their feet. They either stop, which is good but not desired, or they bolt ahead or to the side, which is also not desired. You must help them find a rhythm in the motion first, then add the stimulus, then search for the rhythm again. You must keep going back and forth like this until you have rhythm in the motion and relaxation. In fact, the rhythm in the motion is a great sign of relaxation.

Naturally, of course you will want to start on the ground for your own safety. Teach the horse to travel freely while carrying a saddle, flag, balloons, or any scary thing. Teach them to travel relaxed on the ground, and then advance to riding them as scary things happen around them.

If the horse bolts or runs away, you may have to stop what you're doing and reconnect with your horse. Reset the boundaries *(refer to Step 1)*. If he stops in his tracks instead of bolts, you simply ask him to go again. You have to keep at it for a long time. Don't get frustrated! You'll screw it all up if you do. Frustrated people look like predators. Keep going until you can add the stimulus and keep a rhythm in motion.

Eventually you will get through to the horse. Determination is your key. After a while he'll let you swing that rope, drag that rope, carry that umbrella, or whatever you want. At that point, you will know you have made a big confidence breakthrough with your horse.

Ingela showing confidence in motion while riding Hope bareback and bridle-less while carrying an open umbrella

Christina and Maeve showing total confidence in motion at the local Medieval Celebration.

Special Note

Each speed is a different deal for the horse. Don't assume your horse is going to handle those same stimulants as well at the trot or canter. You've only addressed them while walking. Take your time to address each speed before you put yourself in a situation where you're riding that horse and something scary happens to him.

Our end goal is to create a partnership with our horse based on trust. I want you to begin to trust that your horse will not be reactive to things that happen around him while he's in motion. I'd like for you to trust that you can carry a flag or take off your coat while riding. I'd like you to know you can ride near a busy highway or even ride on a windy day. Once your horse has a firm grasp on your boundaries and has a strong bond with you, you can build his confidence to this stage and enjoy an almost euphoric feeling of a real partnership with your equine friend.

CONFIDENCE BUILDING GOAL 3:
OBSTACLE TRAINING AND THRESHOLD CROSSING

As a part of teaching bravery, we need to address your horse's confidence to approach things and cross over them, like obstacles, trailers, water, and more. Horses often hesitate when it comes to crossing over or passing near scary places or objects. They often hesitate when they're asked to leave their current comfort zone. Those hesitations are what I call "thresholds."

Ingela crossing a small bridge.

In this step (Goal 3) we want to break through some of those hesitations. Hesitation, by the way, is usually a disguise for uncertainty or fear. Until now, most of our training has been about guiding the horse to accept things that happen "to him" instead of things he actually has to interact with, such as a horse trailer or obstacle in the trail or perhaps even other horses in the arena.

To address obstacles and thresholds, you'll use the same basic strategies we used before, such as approach and retreat. You're searching for relaxation. You want your horse to associate that scary thing with a feeling of bravery or at least non-reactive behavior.

Start on the ground where you are safe before trying to ride through scary situations. Teach your horse to cross over ditches, load into trailers, etc. I want you to be able to send them forward when they don't feel they can. I'll use the example of trailer loading to demonstrate what I mean.

Let's say you want to load your horse in the trailer but notice he's resistant and reactive. It's possible that he's not afraid of the trailer, but not likely. Occasionally horses just won't go in, even after years of good loading, because they simply feel uncomfortable in there and they'd rather stay home. I don't blame them. Instead, I help them feel comfortable again. I help them feel good about going with me. I help that horse make a re-association to the trailer that is positive.

Most horses are genuinely scared of going in the trailer. To help a scared horse requires the same basic thinking. Once your boundaries and bond have been established, ask the horse to look at the trailer, then look at you, then back at the trailer. Literally point his nose into the trailer.

Ask him to step toward it and then back away from it by using the same directional tools you used to establish boundaries. This is the same principle of approach and retreat, only instead of the trailer approaching your horse, your horse will be approaching the trailer.

Keep in mind that the hardest thing for the horse to do in these situations is to focus. Help him point toward you or the trailer and nowhere else. When the tension drops, you can invite him to step forward then retreat again. With persistence and good leadership, you can prove to your horse there is nothing to fear. Day by day you will make progress. You'll see your horse crossing small thresholds in the right direction. Reward him for doing so. At a certain stage you'll invite your horse to move closer and stay longer. Then one day you'll even ask your horse to go on a trip with you.

There are many pitfalls to be aware of. And we'll be sure to address all those at the end of the book, but all you need to know right now is that if you approach, retreat, and reward your horse, you will make progress toward crossing thresholds and dealing with scary objects such as a trailer, water, and more.

Our end goal here is to work with each challenge often enough to see your horse work through the hesitations and become free to move forward through scary situations. Ultimately, you will reach those thresholds and your horse will not ask the question "why should I do this" but instead move confidently through on your command. At this point you should feel safe to ride through those same situations. This of course will take practice, but if you set your goals to achieve a task without hesitation, you will get beyond just surviving the scary situations and enjoy a more confident ride each time you go out. Enough practice can deliver moments just like the one you see below.

Rachel riding Diamond through the water.

Trail riding through hell! It's nice to have a horse who doesn't hesitate when asked. Only true confidence can create that kind of horse!

Don training a new horse on a steep hill. Preparing for extreme trails!

Important notes about "thresholds" or what I call "moments of hesitation"

Reward the slightest try

I want to encourage you to notice when your horse tries. Notice the effort. Remember each threshold and every time he or she crosses a threshold. Reward the horse for crossing over and moving closer to the obstacle, stream, trailer, rock, or whatever challenge you face.

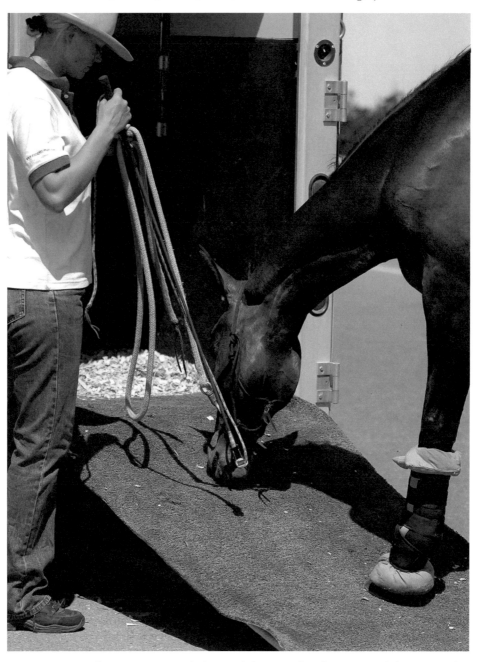

Allow the horse time to process his environment. As long as he's engaged and curious with his nose or feet, allow him (even reward him) for trying.

NEVER punish your horse for NOT moving forward

Be kind and reward-oriented. Be persistent and focused. Don't reward the wrong behavior by releasing pressure or allowing the horse to be out of position, but don't ever punish the wrong behavior either. Punishing a horse creates a "master-slave" like relationship.

This white Arab stallion is showing hesitation around a scary obstacle. With persistence, patience, and practice this same horse will confidently navigate this obstacle!

Don't be frustrated when a horse takes his time getting in or out of a scary situation. Watch for and reward his effort!

Be progressive

Don't continue rewarding the exact same response. After a while it becomes imperative you don't reward the same behavior and instead reward a slight progression in the right direction. Wait to reward a new threshold crossing. Even if your horse just makes it two inches farther, that's considered a threshold crossing. I call that a "progressive try."

With time and practice, there is no obstacle you can't overcome with your horse.

Once you feel like you have a good handle on confidence training you can advance to the next step.

Don't rush, but don't just sit there either. Practice makes perfect! Find the balance between waiting and pushing.

Notice how one foot is making progress toward getting in. Reward each step in the right direction. Measure your progress and ask for a little more each time he makes noticeable changes in his relaxation.

Leadership Step 3 Summary:

Using all the techniques we've learned, I want to encourage you to teach your horse confidence to first tolerate, and ultimately totally relax while any visual, auditory, or tactile stimulus is present, whether your horse is standing still or in motion or navigating obstacles.

LEADERSHIP STEP 4:

BASIC TO ADVANCED SKILL DEVELOPMENT CREATING BALANCE AND ATHLETICISM

I have students who can teach horses to be brave, but don't know much about balance and skill training. Horses can be unconfident with skills just like they can be with obstacles. They can easily get confused with complicated maneuvers. In order to keep your horse's confidence while training skills, remember one simple principle: be reward-oriented in your communication. Approach and retreat techniques with rests and rewards will develop skills in a horse quicker than "drill, drill, drill!" Consequence-oriented trainers can cause a horse to "hate" serving the human. Reward-oriented trainers create positive experiences so the horse wants to be a partner.

How to keep confidence when learning "new skills":

I always say, "It's not *what* you do but *how* you do *what* you do that counts!" What I mean is there are thousands of techniques to achieve skills with horses. I can label a dozen techniques just to teach flying lead changes, and a dozen more just to teach circling or lunging. The point is, *how* you do things matters. You must teach a new skill to a horse the same way you would teach a four-year-old child a new skill: with patience, clear boundaries, a bit of fun included, and lots of breaks. Think of the approach and retreat plan instead of cramming all the information you want your horse to know all in one session.

For example, if you want your horse to learn to move sideways on command:

1. First. Don't assume he knows it – even if he's done it before. They get confused easily. Be a real leader and show some patience.

2. Second. Set your horse up for the game or task by positioning his body for the maneuver, then immediately rewarding him. (Yes!! Reward him for getting into position!) That is key. Too many people want to go to the end product without rewarding the simple steps along the way. Stand out from the crowd and reward the position before the task.

3. Third. Ask with pressure that doesn't offend your horse. If you ask too hard or fast you will lose his confidence. Don't destroy his trust in you by jabbing him inappropriately. When you ask, do it with small amounts of pressure. If you notice after a moment or two that he is distracted, simply ask with more pressure (smoothly). Don't be rough! In dangerous situations, you may have to be firm to stay alive, but in training sessions you must stay patient and soft, using persistence as your guide to teaching.

4. Fourth. Reward your horse for moving, even if it's in the wrong direction at first. Remind him how you care about him. Then, after two attempts, only reward him for moving in the right direction. You must reward your horse often. Every reward for every response he gives counts in the long run when developing new skills.

5. Fifth. Repeat the game over and over until finally you notice he can do it without hesitation. There are thousands of skills horses can learn. You will find some of the most important skills outlined in the next few pages.

THE TRAINING TO BONDING RATIO:

To ensure my horse retains his or her confidence while training I use a very simple model. It's something I teach in all my seminars and clinics. I call it the Training to Bonding Ratio. See the chart below to understand. A perfect balance would be integrating bonding, rewarding, and relaxation time directly into training experiences just like a kindergarten teacher does when introducing new or complex ideas.

Trainers who spend too much time training without integrating bonding time are what I consider to be abusive trainers. Their horses don't last. The attrition rate is horrific.

On the other hand, I see trainers or owners who spend far too little time training and far too much time bonding. Their horses tend to be friendly as long as nothing is required of them. This type of imbalance can be dangerous when common situations require compliance, such as riding, vet care, or trailer loading.

The perfect balance is, of course, right in the middle. Master horse trainers and great leaders always encourage balance, not just physically, but mentally and emotionally as well. You can use this simple model for yourself to judge whether you need more time bonding or more time training. I can say from experience that common problems like catching a nervous horse, can be fixed by spending more time bonding and common problems like bucking can be fixed spending more time training.

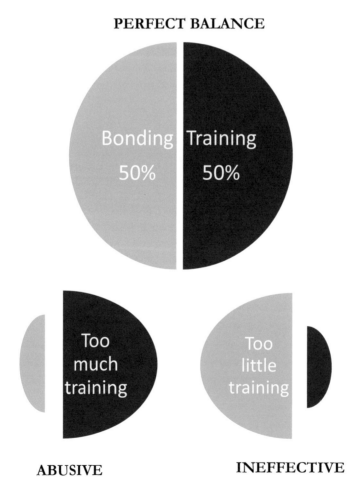

PERFECT BALANCE

Bonding 50% Training 50%

Too much training

Too little training

ABUSIVE   **INEFFECTIVE**

THREE THINGS ALL HORSES NEED TO LEARN

All great horsewomen and horsemen instinctively train three basics skills with their horses. All horses need to learn these skills regardless of training programs you may choose, such as reining, cutting, jumping, dressage, pleasure, trail programs, etc. I've included these three skills in this book because I believe knowing these skills is an integral part of leadership.

Skill number 1: Horses need to learn to be aligned (physically)

The horse's head, shoulders and hips (*the three biggest boney structures*) must learn to travel on the same straight and curved lines around the arena without shifting out of place. Imagine an aerial view of the horse in motion. We want their body parts to line up correctly. Believe it or not this is harder than it looks because horses tend to misalign their body parts often.

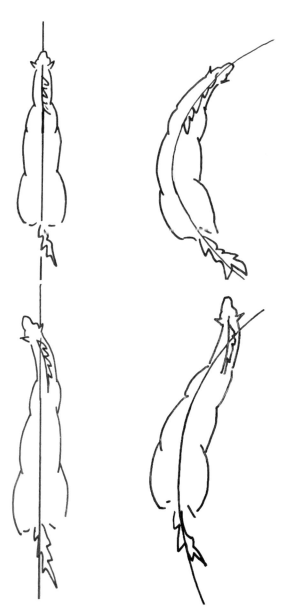

Top 2 drawings show the horse's head, shoulders, hips aligned perfectly on a straight or curved line of travel.

Bottom two drawings show the horse's head, shoulders and hips are not aligned with the direction of travel causing a lack of balance and athleticism.

Opinions differ greatly throughout the horse industry on what a perfectly aligned horse should look like. The key is to remember the word "balance". Try to keep the horse's main body parts moving in harmony to create balance and strength throughout. To correct misalignment, one must use the rein or legs signals (while riding) or rope and stick signals (while on the ground), to guide the necessary body parts into a better place or posture.

Skill number 1 continued: Now imagine a side view of the horse. We also want their poll, withers, and tail head to line up across a horizontal line while traveling or standing still.

A high-headed horse often shows signs of tension or tightness.

An even-headed horse shows signs of relaxation and balance, which can prepare you for higher performance.

A low-headed horse 'can' be better than a high-headed horse for certain purposes, but this can also indicate signs of low interest in the task, distraction, introversion, or even evasion at times.

Alignment training requires awareness and time to develop properly, but leads to exciting physical developments in the horse. They become more athletic, calmer, and more intelligent. They can carry a rider better, stay sounder, and even live longer, because of having good posture in motion.

Ultimately, I want my horses to travel with this basic alignment in all the speeds and transitions between the speeds. I want my horse to be responsive, soft, and light to my hands signals, voice signals, and leg signals while staying non-reactive to all my suggestions.

As I advance, certain aspects of alignment will become more complicated. Those more advanced concepts (such as collection, vertical flexion, haunches and shoulder movements, lateral maneuvers, and more) will be detailed in my next book about skill development. For now, just imagine a collected horse as such:

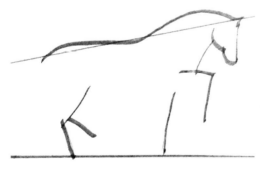

Notice the same basic alignment with the hips, shoulders, and pole of the horse lining up even in high performance training. Contrary to many performance theories, alignment should take priority over power and strength training because proper alignment generates softness and relaxation, which can lead to power without injury or stress.

Skill number 2: Horses need to learn to stay emotionally neutral.

Reading the energy level of your horse is important. You can learn to guide them toward becoming emotionally fit using a simple 0-10 scale.

- **0-4 is a low level of emotional energy (usually viewed as laziness or unresponsive)**

  Strategically, all you must do to invite more energy from the horse is to follow through with your requests with some form of sharp, snappy pressure from a riding crop, stick, rope, spur, etc. ALWAYS remember to be reward-oriented to balance out the pressure you apply *(also see: 'training cycle' on page 91 for the best ways to create sensitivity)*.

- **6-10 is a high level of emotional energy (usually viewed as fearful, stressed, or reactive)**

  Strategically, all you must do to invite less energy from your horse is to redirect the motion of the horse from left to right, forward to backward, backward to forward, or some variation thereof. Redirecting the heightened energy repetitively and randomly can solve lots of emotional flare-ups that occur during training. If all else fails, revert to re-setting boundaries and starting over. Your goal is to find balance in the energy scale.

- **5 is the perfect balance of emotional energy (responsive, alert, but not reactive)**

  Maintaining an even-keeled temperament in a horse is doable by correcting the horse using the strategies written above when they lose their emotional fitness. Also, keep this same scale in mind when training sensitivity to your aids. You don't want a horse reacting to your legs when you ask them to speed up or reacting to your hands when you ask to slow down. You also don't want them to be dull or sluggish to the same requests. We, as leaders, are always looking for the perfect balance of softness, responsiveness, calmness, and willingness. We ultimately want out horses to respond easily to any maneuver, in any direction, at any speed.

Special Note: I don't recommend riding a horse with an energy level below 3 or above 7 on the scale. These horses aren't safe for most riders and need some ground work to regain sensitivity (for horses below 5) and connection/confidence (for horses above 5). Even for professional riders, I encourage ground work to re-establish boundaries and calm, confident behavior from the horse, before riding. Proper ground preparation supports more rideable horses.

Skill number 3: Horses need to learn to stay connected (focused).

Distraction is without any doubt one of the most common problems in horse training. There are thousands of things the horse can pay attention to at any given moment. Our goal is to teach them to pay attention and stay connected to our requests, whether those requests are emotional, physical, or mental. If you look closely you can measure how well a horse is paying attention to you or what you want. I use the simple chart below to measure connection. For mastery level tasks, such as liberty *(playing with no strings attached)* or bridle-less riding *(riding with no reins)* you must develop a strong connection with you and your task otherwise you will have no control and struggle to develop true understanding.

Teaching focus and connection is quite simple. When the horse loses focus, the trainer can use his or her tools (ropes, reins, etc.) to invite the horse to re-align his body with the task. For instance, if the horse won't go in the trailer, check to see if his nose is actually pointed at the trailer.

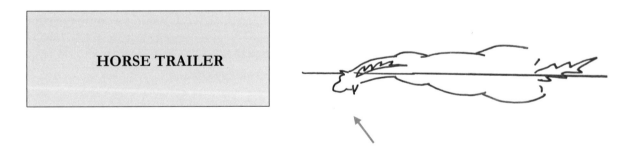

The illustration above shows a horse that is clearly not focused or connected with the idea of going in the horse trailer. By simply realigning his nose and rewarding him, he can easily find what you want. You could replace the horse trailer with a human. Either way, you want your horse to learn to focus and stay connected to you or your goal.

Rewarding the horse every time he lines up with you or a task will encourage better focus. You can reward with treats, kind words, scratching or rubbing, or simple relaxation and rest time while he or she is standing in the correct position. Repetition also encourages focus. Take into consideration that too much variety in training can cause confusion and distress. I can show you a simple cycle I call the "training cycle" that will help you teach the horse to focus and ultimately understand exactly what you want (see "Training Cycle" on next page).

Introducing the TRAINING CYCLE:

The training cycle is a simple way to ensure your horse understands what you want when you ask. Using the training cycle can teach the horse to be sensitive and focused. Here is the TRAINING CYCLE is in five steps:

Step 1: Signal – send a signal to the horse for what you want *(ex: squeeze with your heels to initiate a walk to trot transition)* Now how hold that signal for a few seconds to allow the horse enough time to think. Horses need processing time just like humans. *(3-5 seconds is usually effective)*

Step 2: Support – support your signal with some form of extra energy if your horse doesn't respond *(ex: politely use a riding crop to ensure a response, even if it's the wrong response at first)*

Step 3: Release – once the horse responds, release the signal and support at the same time *(ex: stop tapping with the crop and stop squeezing with your heels)*

Step 4: Reward – let the horse know you appreciate their effort *(ex: say something nice, or pet the horse)*

Step 5: Repeat – repeat step 1-4 until you can get your horse to give you the response you want *without* any hesitation or extra support. Only then do you *truly* know he understands you and is completely focused. Be prepared to take whatever time it takes to ensure understanding, even if you spread your training out over days, weeks, months, or years for certain advanced tasks.

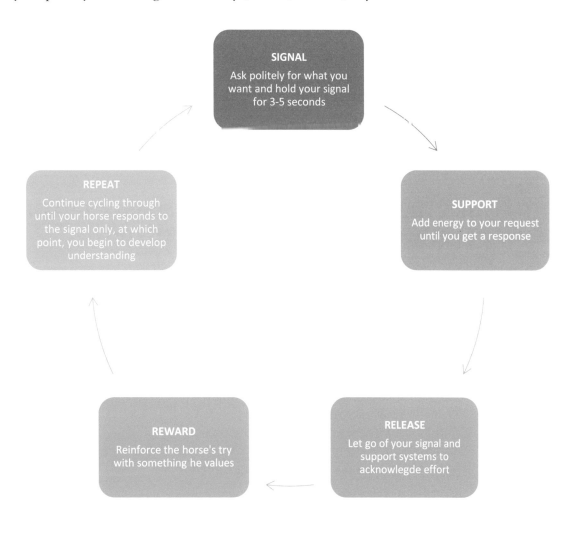

Leadership Step 4 Summary:

Regarding basic to advanced skill development, you are allowed to choose any discipline. What I hope to give you in this book are the important things that make the masters masterful and can turn you into an effective and smart leader, whether you ride Western, English, Traditional, or Natural.

I have hundreds of training exercises for balance and alignment, as well as complete training programs to develop specific skill sets such as foundation riding, liberty, bridle-less riding and advanced riding in all Western or English disciplines. The specifics of these exercises I'll leave for another book. However, the premise here is to remember that you want a confident horse. Not just confident to stimulus but also confident to learning new skills. If you apply all you've learned here, you will not only gain confidence, you will become an effective leader for a partner that trusts and loves your companionship.

While developing your horse, simply remember that you must be a good leader: kind, patient, persistent, firm enough to keep attention. Teach them like you would if you were a kindergarten teacher. Remember your horse has the brain of a four-year-old child. And never be aggressive during learning stages except when boundaries are overstepped and you are in danger of being hurt. In reality, if you find yourself in a position where your horse is trying to buck you off, bite you or kick you, during a training session this may be a sign you have missed some important steps in building his confidence and trust in you as a leader within the first few steps of this book. Never be afraid to revert to your early stages of training to remind your horse about what's most important.

Also, remember this: nearly all problems related to learning new skills stem from confusion and a lack of trust in someone or something in the environment. If you approach skill-building appropriately you will achieve fantastic new levels of competency at no expense to your relationship with your horse *(see principle #7 for why horses don't do what we want)*.

I've seen horses you would think absolutely could NOT achieve the simplest of tasks, and within minutes tune in to me and give me everything I ever wanted. Mastering the skills throughout this book can give you that same level of leadership

I hope I've inspired and informed you well enough to get started. So let's do this! Let's get into this thing we call leadership.

THE FOUR STEP FORMULA FOR BECOMING A LEADER FOR YOUR HORSES - SHORT REVIEW

For the sake of review *(remember... repetition is the mother of skill)*, I want to give you a short version of everything we just covered to make you a better leader with your horse.

1. **Boundaries**

2. **Bonding**

3. **Bravery (confidence training)**
   Preface: What is confidence? Stages of confidence.
   What are the strategies to attain confidence? There are 7
   What are the 3 Goals regarding confidence?
   >   **Goal 1:   Confidence while standing**
   >   **Goal 2:   Confidence in motion**
   >   **Goal 3:   Approaching obstacles and crossing thresholds**

4. **Basic to advanced skill development**

WHAT TO DO NEXT

Connect with your horse and begin developing his trust and skill. Use the four-step leadership formula in the order you've learned. Establish your boundaries and bond with your horse. Look for things he likes, indulge in those things as long as he's respectful of your personal space or boundaries. Then, look for the things that bother him. Teach your horse to be brave, to relax, and to become... confident! Finally, begin teaching the skills you always hoped he or she would have.

As a quick point of reference, during the confidence-building step, I often encourage people to start by using their hands (Tactile Stimulus). Look for areas that horses don't want to be touched. Perhaps there are certain ways in which your horse can't be touched. Think about firm, fast, slow, scratchy, poking – anything that might bother your horse. Then work through those confidence issues using the strategies you've learned while reading this book.

After that, look for noises (Auditory Stimulus) that your horse can't tolerate. Continue to stimulate your horse with those noises until your horse is relaxed.

Finally, look for visual sensations (Visual Stimulus) that overwhelm your horse. Use the list below to give yourself ideas on what bothers horses most. Use the strategies you've learned in this book to develop a confident horse that you can trust and that trusts you.

Once you have mastered all three types of stimuli you will have a completely bombproof horse while standing still! The next step is to teach your horse to tolerate and accept things while in motion. And finally, teach your horse to tolerate and accept things he or she must approach or cross over.

Confidence, in my opinion, is far more important than skill development and should take priority because a confident horse can do anything easier, safer, faster, and better. So, I encourage you to take your time learning all the ways you can stimulate your horse and teach him or her to be brave.

Sometimes, knowing what horses need the most can be difficult. We often find ourselves lacking imagination on what to do next. For that reason, I have listed all the basic things horses are afraid of. Anyone bold enough to make it through the whole list will develop a trust and bond between horse and human that few have ever achieved.

LIST OF THINGS HORSES ARE TYPICALLY AFRAID OF

Tactile: clippers, gloves, plastic bags, tarps, umbrellas, balls in varying sizes touching them, pokes, punches, slaps, unbalanced rider, unbalanced saddle, things dragging over his body, things squeezing his body or legs, things grabbing and not letting go (fence wire or rope), hoses bumping against legs, legs being picked up, uneven footing or unstable footing; being touched on, inside or near ears, eyes, mouth, girth, legs, sheath, utter, flank area, tail, anus, hocks, underside of feet, nails being driven through hoof wall, etc.

Auditory: clippers, zippers, plastic bags, tarps, umbrellas, bouncing balls, ropes dragging, leaves rustling, flags flapping, cars starting or backfiring, tractors, bells, whistles, thundering hoof beats, dogs barking, whips cracking, horns, guns firing or even cocking, ribbons twisting or flapping, balloons popping, trees falling, water running, rocks rolling, noises that rattle, noises that smash, scrape, screech, or go "bang".

Visual: plastic bags, tarps, umbrellas, balls in varying sizes, kites on the ground, kites in the air, flags, flashes of material, flashes of light, flashes of a hand or leg or stirrup, unbalanced rider, unbalanced saddle, things dragging behind them, other horses passing by, ropes swinging or dragging, whips, cars or trucks, ribbons, flowers, stumps, streams, rivers, water hoses, painted lines on the road, uneven footing, jumps, ditches, puddles, horse trailers, rocks, hats, crowds, etc.

NAVIGATING PITFALLS

Understanding your pitfalls is one of the greatest gifts a person can have. Knowing what to do is important, but knowing what to do when things don't go well is just as important. Included in this portion of the book is a list of possible pitfalls: what to be aware of, as well as tips on how to change the way you handle challenging situations or view your horse's behavior.

CAN'T CATCH YOUR HORSE

It's difficult to begin with any training if you can't catch your horse. If you struggle to catch your horse, I want you to know you aren't alone. Even though I didn't put any emphasis on the subject earlier in the book I need you to know how important catching is for the long-term success you want to have. Horses that are hard to catch need to learn to trust you. And if your horse doesn't trust you to enough to be caught, then you have no right to engage in technical training. Here is one simple way you can earn their trust before you ever put a halter on.

Simple rules to remember: Don't stress your horse with excessive running around. There is no need for it. To be successful with catching, one must be patient, repetitive, and kind. Timing and positioning are everything when it comes to mastering the game of catching "uncatchable" horses. Let me explain in a way that you'll never forget.

Step 1: Encourage movement from your horse as long as he's *not* looking at you. This causes the horse to feel discomfort for not paying attention. DO NOT punish him or her for leaving. Simply discourage a lack of focus by **politely** and calmly keeping him in motion until he looks at you again. At which point you will back away.

Politely encourage motion as long as he's <u>not</u> looking at or facing you.

Step 2: Encourage your horse to look at you by physically backing away every time he looks in your direction. This simple maneuver acts like a vacuum and literally draws the horse closer. If he or she turns away from you simply revert to step one. If he or she freezes while looking at you and refuses to come any closer, then you can quietly approach him. Master horsemen have a variety of different techniques to enhance these two basic concepts, but all you need to know for now is to stick with step one and step two. Over time, with daily practice, your horse will become a "pro" at being caught and he'll even look forward to seeing you when you come by.

Encourage your horse to look at you by walking or backing away when he does look at you. This rewards the horse and acts like a vacuum, drawing him closer.

When you finally connect, don't be in a hurry to halter your horse. Take your time and be kind with your body language. If he continues to be skeptical of your touching or haltering him, simply revert to what you've just learned and continue until he can stand calmly while you halter him.

CAN'T GET YOUR HORSE TO RESPOND TO BOUNDARIES

Often in the beginning, horses don't respond well to boundaries because they simply don't know what you want. They will either push into your space, which makes it nearly impossible to learn anything, or they pull away in a reactive manner, which makes learning just as hard. Think of a classroom. There is a certain distance the children have from the teacher. Without that set distance learning becomes difficult because attention can be easily scattered. Fixing non-responsive horses is easy with one simple concept. Pressure motivates and release teaches! Pressure motivates the horse to move, and if you release at the right time, your horse will learn exactly what you want. Repetition will create even more understanding.

Pressure can be applied in dozens of different ways. So far all we've talked about in this book is wiggling the rope to illicit a backup from your horse, but there are more techniques you can apply. You can use your hands and literally push the horse backward. You could use a flag and drive your horse backward by waving the flag toward him. You can use verbal cues to support what you want too.

The principles behind movement are simple. If he/she doesn't respond, increase the pressure until he does. Refer to the "training cycle" earlier. If he does respond release the pressure and reward your horse.

Some horses aren't as dull as others. Some horses become quite reactive when asking for boundaries. Fixing reactivity is quite easy as well. Simply apply less pressure. That's it. Use their natural energy and invite them to slow down mentally and physically by asking with less pressure to do what you want. Don't forget to be repetitive, because repetition is the mother to all skill.

One other key to setting up good boundaries is to remember NOT to move your own feet. If you move to accommodate your horse, he or she will never learn to respect your suggestions. The principle is to teach your horse to move away from and around you, not the other way around. One simple example of this is when I see people attempting to get on a horse from a mounting block. Often, if the horse won't stand next to the mounting block, the rider will come down and lead the horse back into place. Principally, you shouldn't approach the problem by retreating from the mounting block because that implies you are moving to accommodate your horse instead of moving him to accommodate you. Remember you are the leader after all, and to retain that leadership you must stay grounded, move less and become more stable, making it easier for your horse to read what you want.

Novice trainers move their feet too much when training on the ground; master trainers stay centered. I encourage you to do the same. Move with your horse from time to time, but when setting up boundaries, stay grounded and relatively close to your starting point. Only after boundaries are clearly set up and the horse is sensitive to your early suggestions should you start bonding with him or her. During the bonding and early confidence training stages, your rolls literally reverse. You want your horse to stay grounded while you move around him.

Regarding your body language try to remember this:

- Boundaries: You stay grounded while the horse moves away and around you on command,

- Bonding: Your horse stays grounded while you move in to show him you care.

- Bravery: Your horse stays grounded while he learns to accept scary things happening around him.

- Basic to Advanced training: You stay grounded when necessary and move with your horse when necessary (depends on the activity).

TROUBLE READING THE EXPRESSIONS:
THINKING THE HORSE IS DOMINANT INSTEAD OF FEARFUL

Occasionally I see people address what they think is a dominance issue, such as a horse striking or biting, when in actuality the horse may be expressing a real fear. The horse feels he or she has no other options. Remember the story earlier of the rejected thoroughbred mare. Everybody thought she was mean, or nasty. I knew she was scared. I still firmly established boundaries, but I knew the underlying issue was fear and not dominance. In knowing that, I adjusted my strategy accordingly. Once I firmly established my safe space (boundaries) I developed a bond and began teaching confidence slowly. I never made the horse feel bad or guilty for reacting the only way it knew how. I simply reset the boundaries every time she stepped too close.

Ingela is showing no frustration toward the reactive horse because she knows it's not dominant behavior from the horse. If it were, she'd revert to re-setting the boundaries.

If you were in this person's shoes, you may begin to feel upset toward the horse, try to remember the horse is NOT being naughty, but simply reacting to fearful emotions about odd stimulus. In this case, it was bareback riding.

THINKING THE HORSE IS RELAXED AND INADVERTENTLY QUITTING TOO SOON

I see people quit too early all the time. They think the horse has made a lot of improvement and then cease training. They reward their horse by putting them away, when in reality the horse has just made it to Stage 2: Tolerate. This is a good <u>resting</u> point, but not a good <u>quitting</u> point. It's better to have some more signs of relaxation *(such as head lowering, eyes softening, smoother breathing patterns, licking and chewing)* before quitting. You want your horse to have a positive response, not just a respectful response to the stimulus. Eventually, with enough training you will achieve total and complete confidence.

Notice the tension in the horse's expression. Both horses are at stage 2: Tolerate.

The trainer should most certainly NOT quit yet. More training and time doing what she is currently doing will help the horse lower her head and soften around the eyes and ears, which are two of many signs that tell us the horse is beginning to gain more confidence.

THINKING THE HORSE IS READY AND CONTINUING (GETTING EXPLOSIVE BEHAVIOR)

It's easy to assume that once a horse can do a "little" they should be able to handle a "lot," but in truth, you have to move slower than this. If a horse can handle one thing while walking, you don't want to assume it will work while trotting. Your horse handling something coming toward him slowly doesn't mean he can handle it coming quickly. Each game is different.

Often people mistake Stage 2 (Tolerate) with relaxation and continue to challenge their horse with more progressive obstacles, only to cause extreme reactivity in their horse. The horse reacts simply because the horse isn't ready.

I've seen people work their horse on the ground, then get on to ride only to have the horse rear and flip over backward, in some cases killing the rider. This happens because the rider thinks the horse is relaxed, when in fact the horse is only barely tolerating the stimulus. Proceed carefully and ask the horse to yield from time to time to ensure he or she isn't frozen or introverted. In a situation like this I always do more ground work. I don't assume the horse is ready until he proves he's ready by standing quietly when asked and moving rhythmically when asked. I don't want to see any hesitation or reactive behavior as I prepare to ride.

This rider assumed the horse was ready and found out the hard way that he was not. More ground tests with the horse carrying other objects at speed would teach the horse not to buck or rear with odd stimulus, like a new rider on his back.

THINKING THE HORSE IS AFRAID, WHEN HE'S SIMPLY DISTRACTED

Once you develop an eye for distracted expressions, they become extremely obvious. Horses can be excited and seem scared, but in reality, they may be excited and simply distracted. It's important to help them focus on you as their leader first, then on the tasks at hand. I don't allow my horse to look around the place nervously whether they are scared *or* distracted. I consistently re-align my horse to encourage focus. I want my horse to see me as his or her leader, and of course I also give him time to see the obstacles we're going to focus on as well because I want more than robotic behavior.

Tecate is clearly distracted; he is showing no signs of fear, but instead disregarding his rider as not important. Luckily for Christina, he is respectful enough to stand still.

Christina is not worried about Maeve's expression because she knows that her horse is clearly distracted at a low level and not fearful or out of control; but notice she still has hold of the reins, just in case.

100

THINKING THE HORSE IS BEING OBSTINATE WHEN HE'S JUST REACTING TO PRESSURE

Similar to the first pitfall, I see people mistreat their horses because they assume the horse is being stubborn. What looks like stubbornness is often a form of fear. If you smash or beat on your horse for being stubborn, you'll make things worse. As a basic rule of thumb, work with "approach and retreat techniques" while staying reward-oriented, instead of "fear, force, and intimidation" techniques. The latter techniques are strictly consequence-oriented and no animal on the planet wants a leader who is consequence-oriented.

If you think your horse is being obstinate, you may feel like taking your own emotions out on the horse.

If you think he/she's just reacting to stimulus or expressing confusion, you will be more likely to remain calm like Ingela; and you can see how it pays off in the last picture.

Try to give your horse the benefit of the doubt and express patience rather than frustration.

MISREADING THE ENERGY:
THINKING THE HORSE IS RELAXED WHEN SHE/HE'S STILL TIGHT

Sometimes the horse looks relaxed on the exterior, but inside he's still tense. Be sure to look a little deeper. Look for tightness in the muscles. Look for faster than normal heart rate and breathing. These things are subtle, but still visible. Look for hardness in their eyes or tension in their jaw. A clenched jaw, for instance, or a tight-set tail, are both signs of tension.

  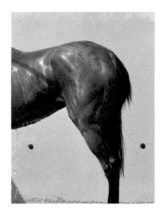

Tight lips, Tight ears, or Tight tail

Simple little tests like picking up the tail or touching the ears or lips can tell you if the horse is "frozen" or truly relaxed! And of course, when you notice the horse is NOT relaxed it means more time training in those areas will be required for your safety and your horse's safety/sanity.

ALLOWING THE HORSE TO FLEE AND INJURE HIMSELF

Occasionally, there may come a time when the horse's energy is too high. One strategy is to allow the horse to "blow" off some steam. Let them go, let them run around the arena and see everything for themselves. This is an effective strategy when the energy is high, because you can stay out of harm's way… but when the energy is *way too* high you can actually set your horse up for injury.

Horses can do what I call "right brain blindness." The instinctive right hemisphere of the brain takes over and they fail to see the obstacles in front of them. You may have seen this before. Every time a horse runs through a fence, or crushes into people or walls. It's because they can't actually *see* those obstacles (not clearly anyway). Everything is fuzzy and all they think about is freedom. They

can literally kill themselves in an attempt to find safety. Be sure to read the energy and decide for yourself if you should allow your horse to freely check out his space, or gain some control by staying connected with ropes.

Sometimes when the energy is too high I will still allow him to check things out, but I purposely stay connected to the horse with a halter and long rope. This way I can contain the right brain blindness better when it shows up.

Allowing him to move, but containing his movement so he won't jump out, as he thought about earlier.

MISREADING THE PRIORITIES "BOUNDARIES FIRST"

Problems arise by allowing the horse to come too close or pull away too much. I can tell you how important boundaries are, but you have to remember for yourself. Boundaries are the first port of call. Many times, people skip step one in the 4-step formula and try training confidence or building rapport before setting up clear boundaries. They assume the horse is respectful, then with little provocation the horse jumps on top of the person or bolts away. This horse clearly does not know the boundaries set up by the leader and is a hazard to himself and the people around him.

Don't allow your horse to invade your space uninvited. It's not appropriate. It's a nice gesture for the horse to want to come close, but he can hurt you in less than a second of time. Wait a few days before you start allowing the horse to come in close on his own. In fact, in most of my seminars I ask people to wait a few months before they allow this. You build the relationship by building rapport and respect together. Too much rapport without respect will ruin your relationship, and of course vice versa.

Also, don't allow your horse to pull away. You don't want your horse to learn to bolt away. You don't want a habit to form any time he or she feels scared. In the event my horse does get away, which can happen, I simply drop what I'm doing, go catch my horse, and start again slowly. I don't have to deal with this very often. Mostly because when I see it's about to happen, I abandon the confidence-building games and go right to re-establishing boundaries.

Remember the boundaries are "not too close" and "not too far away". There are limitations to my horse's movement. If I make those limitations a priority I will be more successful. I don't want to have to chase my horse around the arena trying to train confidence. I want him to see I'm his leader. Like a good parent managing a fearful child, simply setting some ground rules and progressing slowly may be your key to success. When things are prioritized with boundaries before confidence building, the chances of succeeding are much greater.

This horse is clearly pushing through boundaries. The only and most important thing to do in situations like this is put a fence between you and teach the horse boundaries until he or she understands the value of respecting someone else's space.

Ingela is carefully but assertively re-establishing boundaries. Remember; don't try to bond with an animal who wants to kill you, or one who's too distracted or nervous to pay attention to you. Establish leadership early and you won't find yourself in these kinds of situations. Professionals like Ingela and myself often end up correcting boundary issues with difficult horses like this beautiful athlete. Sometimes the horses we work with have either never been touched by humans or humans have abused the relationship and the horse is fighting to preserve his life and dignity. Occasionally horses become difficult because humans have allowed pushy behavior from the horse for too long. Don't be afraid to correct your horse's pushy behavior early on and reap the benefits as you continue to train and bond with your equine partner.

MISREADING THE DISTRACTION/CONCENTRATION LEVEL

A typical mistake many make when working with horses is to focus on getting the feet to do what you want and forgetting about where the horse's eyes and ears are focused. It's important to remember you are dealing with a live breathing animal in an unnatural environment. Don't be afraid to look at them. Look into their eyes and see if they look back. A relaxed horse is not afraid of looking at a human. A tense horse is afraid to look or sometimes, may not even be afraid, but so distracted by other things that looking at you is not a priority. Help your horse to focus, not just mechanically move around. Sometimes people will assume their horse is relaxed because his feet aren't moving; but look at the rest of his body. Where is he looking? What is he thinking?

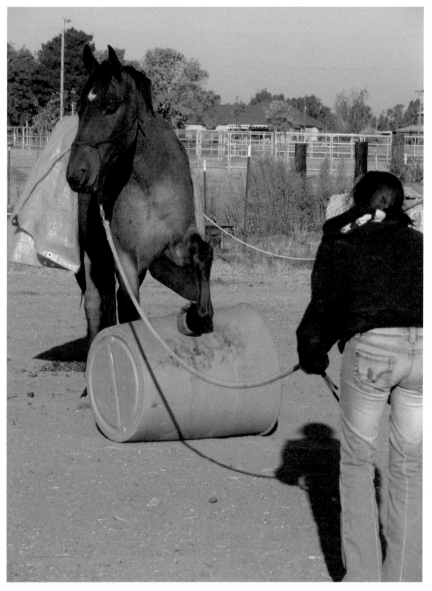

This horse is clearly confident, yet also clearly distracted. Sometimes people misinterpret this as fearful behavior from the horse and slow everything down rather than quickly grab the horse's attention and carry on. Distraction is not such a big deal until it becomes a big deal.

Addressing distraction early is helpful and easily done by simply bringing him back to face you or the task at hand, by asking politely with your voice or softly tugging on the rope.

MISREADING THE FEAR ENERGY LEVEL

Sometimes thinking the horse is only a little bit afraid instead of immensely afraid can be an easy mistake to make. Don't assume that some *"little"* thing to you is such a little thing to your horse. In reality, your horse may require more time and training to overcome seemingly small obstacles.

You can't always prevent horses from reacting, but when they do, it can be a signal that their energy level is high and you don't need to ask with more pressure, but simply ask for what you want by using smaller pressures and more rewards, repeating until you get the desired outcome. There is rarely a need to escalate the energy level.

Also, don't assume you can do everything in one session. Related to this is when someone assumes their horse is being stubborn when in actuality they are being afraid. Recently I helped a wild burro get into a trailer. He'd been shoved in before, but never asked. So, I asked him in, patiently guiding him with the halter and lead. He resisted and pulled back. Strategically, I would simply hold my ground, but not add any extra pressure. An hour and a half later he entered the trailer completely confident and willing.

If at any time, I assumed he was being stubborn and applied inappropriate pressure on him, he would have gone from fearful to fighting and what took an hour and a half would have taken two days. But worse than that, he would have lost trust in me as a leader. He would have seen me only as a dictator with no feeling for him or what he needs. Don't assume resistance is belligerence. Resistance is usually a sign of hesitation and hesitation is usually related to a lack of confidence or trust.

Simply taking more time, re-setting boundaries, ensuring a true bond is present, and teaching confidence is the key to getting exactly what you want.

ASSUMING SOME SCARY OBJECT IS THE PROBLEM WHEN IN FACT THE PROBLEM *MAY* BE ABOUT THE "FLASH" OF AN OBJECT

Imagine walking through a grassy field when a bird suddenly flaps his way up past your horse's belly into the sky. Your horse spooks and you fall off. What's important to remember here is that *occasionally* it's not about the object, but instead it's about the *flash* of the object. Your horse isn't afraid of birds. Your horse is afraid of something flashing up by his belly. You can train him to handle things randomly flashing up by his belly or any other part of his body using the techniques we talked about before called "flash training." Using a white flag or plastic bag tied to a string, you can randomly fly the object off the ground and around your horse's body to simulate the bird flying up. Over time your horse stops reacting and you have created a more "bombproof" horse.

Sweet T and Ready 4 playing in the arena, when suddenly, a ball they've seen 100 times before bounces or flashes in their field of vision.

MISREADING FEAR OR RELUCTANCE FOR REAL PHYSICAL LIMITATIONS

While working toward developing skills, a person may think the horse is being resistant and afraid of a task when physically he may be hurting or even afraid of further injury. On rare occasions, I see horses resist jumping or faster speeds in regular flat work due to physical limitations. They may be sore or lame, but don't show it physically. It can look like a lack of confidence or hesitation, when in actuality, both may be present because when a horse is sore they are both uncomfortable and hesitant. Usually you can spot a physical limitation with a head bobbing or a limping leg, but on those rare cases you can't actually *see* the lameness, you still shouldn't rule out lameness. It's difficult to see, but with a trained eye you start to notice certain types of soreness. If you're not sure, ask your vet. You want to keep an eye out and *not* make any assumptions when being the leader your horse deserves.

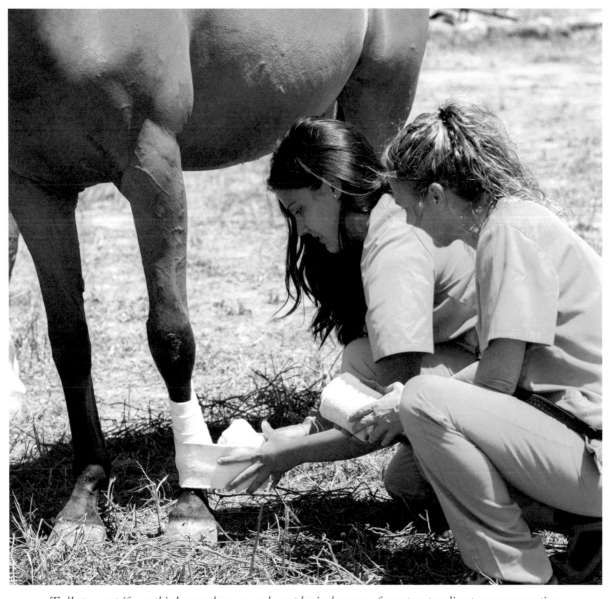

Talk to a vet if you think your horse may have physical reasons for not responding to your suggestions.

NOT CONTINUING THE PATTERN

Don't assume you've fixed the problem; that you've reached the bottom of the issue in one session. To resolve an issue may take much more time than most people are willing to commit! Certain issues will take more time and more training sessions than other issues. I've seen this happen thousands of times. We think, "I've fixed it!" then come back the next day to see it's still broken. Remember that horses need many sessions in a row to really understand something. As we talked about before, to make progress you have to advance from getting your horse to tolerate things to finally relax with things. Don't be worried that in some cases this can take months, and with some challenging tasks even longer.

GETTING FRUSTRATED (KNOW YOUR TIMELINES)

Don't assume you can achieve everything at once. Many people get frustrated with how long things take, and then take it out on your horse. Don't worry if things take a while to get through. Building confidence is like building a home. Take your time to do it right and don't get upset when the house isn't finished on the first day. Remember, frustrated people look like predators! If you look like a predator your horse will not trust you.

Some things surprise me when I'm training. I've seen horses get over some big challenges very quickly – quicker than I thought. Then on the flip side, I've seen horses take days to get over something small. I don't assume my timelines anymore. I take the time it takes. No pressure!

EXPRESSING THE WRONG ENERGY TOWARD YOUR HORSE

Remember, being *too* nice or lenient when boundaries need to be set is an important leadership fault. Depending on your personality, you will find it easy or perhaps hard to be nice to your horse. But keep in mind being nice isn't always the most appropriate behavior. If your horse is pushing you over and dominating all the safe space around you because he's scared of something he sees, remember…this is not the time to be sweet. Instead, be a leader! Establish clear boundaries, then be nice after he's calmed down, focused, and respecting your space. If a horse is in a panic about his environment, don't rub him and reward him for feeling that way. Instead, set up your boundaries and wait for him to relax; then rub him and reward him for being relaxed. You'll be amazed at the difference this subtle timing makes.

On the flip side: Don't be too fast when genuine fear shows up. Also, depending on your personality, you will find it easy to be too fast with your horse. Sometimes the horse is genuinely scared. Don't push the thresholds on him. Don't blast him over thresholds. Give the horse time to think and be reward-oriented in your training. If you're being quick, just ask yourself, "Is my horse trusting me?"

MOVING TOO FAST OR TOO MUCH PRESSURE (OVER FACING)

People with a lot of bravado seem to want to accomplish everything at once and often "over face" the horse. They put too much pressure on, too fast, with no other ways for the horse to figure out what he or she is supposed to do. I've seen people tie flags or aluminum cans to their horse's mane or tail. I've see people go enter cowboy mounted shooting competitions without preparing their horse. I've seen people enter the starting gates on the racetrack for the first time on the first race ever. Don't do that because it's not fair to the horse.

Be the kind of leader that sets things up slowly. Remember you're dealing with a four-year-old brain. Animal behavior scientists agree you can't push a horse too hard or you will create a traumatic experience. If you do, you'll be spending more time rebuilding trust and rapport than you will be progressing to new heights.

Both these extreme situations could be avoided with more ground work and smaller, easier tasks done thoroughly, rather than in haste.

MISREADING THE ENVIRONMENTAL CONTROLS: FOOTING, OTHER PEOPLE, ETC.

Working with a horse in an unsafe area is hazardous to both you and the horse. What are examples of unsafe areas? No fences, gravel ground, sharp edges in the corral, too many people, etc. Take for example a young lady who tried the "flooding" technique on the gravel driveway at home. Her horse reared over backward and completely shredded her rear end and hind legs. The horse took two years to make a full recovery from that split-second mistake.

Also, take for example a trainer I know who, while in the arena, got too close to the fence with an extreme horse. When the horse reared over backward he split his head on a fence post and died instantly. Be careful in your selection of footing, obstacles, and fences. Be safe for you and your horse.

Many accidents can be avoided by looking closely at your environment before leading your horse into it.

MISTIMING THE "WINDOW OF OPPORTUNITY"

When you feel like taking the next progressive step in your training, be careful you don't get yourself hurt because the window of opportunity for progress may be long-gone. The window of opportunity is a small amount of time the horse will focus on you or the task. If you miss the window, you won't be able to progress and you'll have to try and re-open another window.

For example, let's say I'm training a colt for that first ride. Let's say, I help him become confident walking, trotting, and cantering with me on the ground while he carries the saddle. He looks great and looks ride-able. He's mastered the ground work after several attempts and looks ready for the next step. Then...my phone rings. I'm temporarily distracted. I decide to let my horse rest while I talk to my friend for ten minutes. Finally, I hang up and attempt to get on my horse. But what happens next is the crazy part.

The window of opportunity for getting on his back is gone. My horse isn't concentrating on being relaxed anymore. He's become tense again even though he hasn't moved a step. If I get on *now* I would be putting my life at risk because he's not focused anymore. He could be focused internally and temporarily unaware of his environment and may have even completely forgotten what happened just ten minutes before. Who knows what he *may* do with all the built-up tension. If I just assume he's well and carry on without first asking for smaller responses, I could get hurt.

When trying to progress to a new step, pay attention to the window of opportunity. You have to allow rest time and reward time, but if you wait *too* long you'll lose the concentration and risk undoing what good has been done. If you *do* miss the window, simply go back a step and ensure he's still concentrating and relaxed. Then take advantage of that new window and progress to the next step. Consider the window of opportunity concept often, especially in regard to riding.

Fabricio had control and confidence a minute ago, but assumed the connection was still intact when he started asking again. His mistake was not checking in with smaller requests before trying out harder things. His window of opportunity had closed and now he's in a more dangerous situation.

Rachel asking Cloe to canter just a little bit too early. The window of opportunity was not yet open. For a confident rider like Rachel it's not a big deal, but for a novice rider it's important to ask for a smaller request and get many "Yes" answers before asking for big requests like the canter.

MISJUDGING YOUR OWN SKILL

A common pitfall I dare say I've made dozens of times in my career is misjudging my own skill level. It's easy to do, but the lessons you learn will live with you forever. To avoid this pitfall, one must learn to read the horse's energy, athleticism, and patterned behaviors. Reading the horse takes practice, but over time you can start seeing how some situations call for more qualified persons to address them.

If you find yourself in a situation that is "over your head" so to speak, simply revert to the most primary parts of this program. Boundaries first! Always! Then reach out for help as soon as you can find someone more qualified you can trust.

Just to be clear however, most people don't have the skills we've talked about in this book; but once they learn these basic leadership principles and skills, they become more efficient than most everybody else around them.

If you start small, stay safe, and begin with boundaries, bonding, bravery, and basic training, in that order, (successfully transitioning only after mastering those basics) you will eventually succeed no matter what discipline you choose to follow.

Don't get caught in a situation that could lead to a hospital visit. Your life is worth doing smaller steps or finding help to take bigger steps.

RELEASING TOO SOON

Under pressure, people often feel or think they are doing the wrong thing.

For example: if your horse won't cross a stream when you squeeze with your legs to go, you can feel like you're doing something wrong. When this happens people often tend to release their leg pressure and stop what they are doing to re-assess what to do next. The problem is that you released your legs *before* your horse even responded to you. If you continue to do this, your horse will think that your legs don't mean go. In fact, they don't mean anything.

It's important to ask for a response before you let go of your asking aids: halter pressure, rein pressure, or leg pressure. If you release at the wrong time, your horse learns the wrong thing. It's simple to remember, but hard to implement when your horse is being reactive. Usually all you have to do is ensure you get some positive response toward your goal. You don't have to get perfection; you just have to get progress before you release the pressure. You don't need more pressure usually. You just have to hold the pressure until you get some positive response. You only need more pressure if your horse has already learned that your legs or reins don't mean anything.

If he releases now the horse will think to pull harder to get the release next time. If he holds just long enough, until the horse comes back, the horse will learn to respond to the halter rather than pull on it next time. Releasing at the right time helps you make progress. Repetition of the skill helps the horse truly understand what you want!

CREATING A DULL HORSE

I often hear my students in the early stages of training, tell me concerns about their horse becoming "desensitized" and therefore dull to their communication. I felt it was fitting to put this comment last because it does address a real concern.

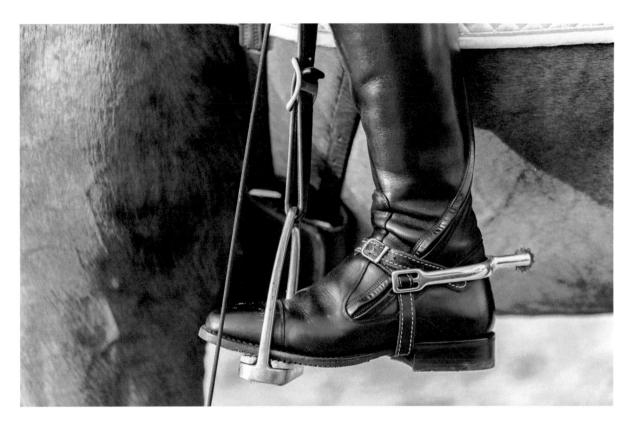

First, I want you to know that I believe you literally cannot do *too* much desensitization with your horse; that is... if you're desensitizing the right things. But if you inadvertently cause your horse to become dull to your suggestions because you've over-trained his relaxation, then we have a slightly different problem.

Bravery or confidence training is about taking away reactivity to scary things. It's NOT about de-sensitizing signal cues. Many non-natural trainers use the horse's reactivity to propel them over jumps and into competition. They seem to love the heightened expression of the horse and can even get higher points from some judges. *We* don't want to do that. It's simply not fair to the horse or safe for any rider.

However, in the process of training confidence you *can* inadvertently train "over-relaxation" and with some horses this converts to dullness.

Here's what to do if it happens to you:

Let's say your horse doesn't react to anything anymore. Let's say you have practiced with every type of stimulus and you literally can't get a rise out the horse. You can't spook your horse no matter how hard you try. But now... you can't get him to move when you want either. This is what some people are afraid of happening. But you needn't fear. In this scenario, you simply shift your focus back to creating sensitivity to what you want instead of what you don't want.

Here's what I mean. I don't want my horse to be sensitive to a balloon flying up in the air. I do, however, want him to be sensitive to my leg pressure if I'm asking for a yield or my hand pressure if I'm asking for a stop or turn. When my horse becomes dull to my suggesting aids I simply shift my focus away from confidence building and back to control.

Step #4 in the four-step formula (basic to advanced training) is designed to start building a horse's skill, sensitivity to your signals, and athleticism. In this step, you have to start asking for *things*. You have to apply pressure in a way that will cause the horse to respond, but not become reactive. This becomes a whole other topic to deal with, but essentially you must play games with your horse by applying hand, leg, or stick pressure to cause the horse to move, and then reward the horse with a release and bonding.

To train sensitivity for any specific task you want, you simply must have a clear objective. Once *you know exactly what you want, you can stimulate your horse with pressure from your legs or hands*, and finally release when he moves in the right direction. By doing this you'll create the responses you want from your horse

Here's a simple principle to remember: Pressure motivates the horse and the Release teaches. Rewards reinforce the behavior you want and Repetition causes true understanding. For review I encourage you to look back to the **Training Cycle diagram on page 91.**

Horses can learn to do anything you want if you apply your leadership principles and stay reward-oriented. Ultimately, you can do anything too, if you apply these same principles to your own life and stay reward-oriented with yourself.

From Information to Inspiration and Action

It's time to face the real world now. You have the information you need to succeed with horses as a leader they can trust. Today, take a step out your door toward your horses with a new perspective on who you are and what your horse needs. Don't be afraid to take on new challenges using your boundaries and bonding to guide you and your horse toward new skills. I'll be there anytime you need. Just pick up this book and review each step. If you feel you want more, reach out and contact me or my team for more support.

Someone I know and admire once put great faith in my ability to learn, grow, and master the skills I need to communicate effectively with horses and humans. Today I'm putting that same faith in you! I believe in you! I believe you can do anything you've ever dreamed up, including things unrelated to horses. Just in case you don't have enough faith in yourself to get going, take a little bit of mine with you. Soon... success will shine on you in any endeavor you choose.

APPENDIX

SAFETY

Technically there are many things a horse trainer or rider needs to know. But basically, there are only a few safety techniques. As we've talked about throughout the book, establishing boundaries is one of the biggest factors to having a successful day with your horse. Anytime you feel afraid for yourself, remember to reestablish the boundaries and you'll become safer almost instantly.

However, these strategies don't always convert perfectly to riding. So far, we've talked mostly about ground training and confidence building. When it comes to riding, you are now asking the horse to do things without the visual aids of the ground person. New skills will have to be developed to be successful. Set yourself up for success on the ground first. This will minimize reactivity from the horse while riding. However, in some instances, no matter how well you set up, your horse will still react while you're riding. Here are a few safety tips to keep in mind while riding.

TIP 1: FACE THE PROBLEM

Imagine riding your horse down the trail and suddenly your horse is spooked by a noise coming from behind him. The safest thing to do is quickly ask your horse to turn and face the challenge. They don't have to move toward the scary object, but simply face it. This can give you time to reassess if you should progress toward it or move away. If the horse's energy is too high, you may want to get off. The last thing you want to happen is to have your horse rear up or bolt away with you dragging on the ground. Facing the obstacle can give you time to think and give your horse the impression you have things under control.

In certain circumstances, you simply can't turn around. Perhaps the trail is too narrow. In this situation, you are best to simply try to contain the problem or get off.

Tip 2: Try to Contain the Problem

Containing the problem means you do what you can to keep your horse from exploding. Maybe just pulling back on the reins to slow your horse or back up is enough. If you can't face the problem, at least try to contain your horse's energy and keep him heading in a safe direction. When all else fails, get off because that way you live to tell your stories.

Tip 3: Move in Arching Lines Instead of Straight Lines

Part of containing the problem can sometimes involve moving your horse in arching lines instead of straight lines. By moving in arching lines instead of straight lines you will gain more control of the horse's movement. The basic principle here is that a horse moving in a straight line is more powerful than a horse moving on a curved line or in small circle. If you can cause your horse to bend slightly instead of "power up" and shoot forward you will be more able to contain the situation.

TIP 4: GET OFF

You can't always stay safe with horses. That's just the reality we face. If you get in a car, you risk your life to a certain degree. It's even more risky to ride a horse. But the good news is that less people die riding horses than driving cars. The risk we usually face as riders is broken bones and head injuries – which are still not very appealing! So in most cases I recommend you don't ride in dangerous situations, especially where your options are limited, such as tight spaces and narrow trails where falling a long distance is a possibility.

Limit your risk of injury for you or your horse by setting things up in advance for safety; but in case you *do* find yourself losing control of your horse, getting off and re-establishing leadership from the ground just may be the best option. I personally use this option often. I have no pride issues when it comes to staying alive. I'm a confident person in my own right, but even more confident when I have things under control. I invite you to learn the same confidence and become more aware of situations that could be dangerous.

TIP 5: GET HELP

In the event you get off and you still can't get control of your horse, you should consider contacting a professional for help with your horse. You may need someone to teach your horse how to be more confident and respectful in scary situations.

HOW TO REACH ME

This book can create a new learning curve for you and your horse. I hope your reading it helps you on your journey to being safer, smarter, and better in general with horses. In the event, you need more help and want to learn more about confidence training and skill building with horses, I invite you to reach out to me.

Contact Information:

don@masteryhorsemanship.com
www.MasteryHorsemanship.com
406-360-1390

Other Products

Dreams with Horses Written by Rachel Jessop

Enroll yourself in this fantastic fictitious story depicting Rachel's real life challenges and experiences. Share in her journey as a satiny white stallion guides her through emotional healing and personal strength.

The struggles and triumphs that Rachel encounters on her adventure will shine a light on your own life's journey, inspiring and encouraging you to reignite your own dreams. Join her on the ride and discover yourself how to live where nothing holds you back.

www.dreamswithhorses.com

Success Pathways Coaching

Private Coaching from across the globe.

Success Pathways is a private, monthly coaching platform, where video and conference calls propel our students forward toward their own goals.

Learn more at:

www.masteryhorsemanship.com

Clinics and Demonstrations

1,2 and 3 day courses at facilities around the world.

For information about booking a clinic or demonstration near you contact:

don@masteryhorsemanship.com

Testimonials about Don Jessop

I looked at my journal from this past month, and the last thing I wrote was, "I'm beginning to believe..." Nothing is more powerful than what we believe in our hearts to be true. You are really, seriously, amazingly helping me. Thank you!
- Karen VA

Thank you, Don! I had the best ride I've had in years! Simple, straightforward, and relaxed.
- Lori CO

It is rare to find an instructor who is knowledgeable and wise about what knowledge a student most needs, communicates clearly and effectively, and has such a kind and compassionate manner of teaching and connecting with humans and horses. Thank you, Don
- Kendra SC

This note is to THANK YOU for your astute help with what was for me, one of my horse's most difficult issues. You made it so easy.
-Bob CA

Hi Don, thank you for all the help you gave to me and my horse. We'd been working on her canter issues/confidence this summer and it seems as if everything just jelled perfectly for us at your clinic. You've given me some great info and techniques to use with her and myself and we put them to use today and achieved some very soft canters both on line and astride! Thanks again.
-Mary VT

Hi Don- I had the BEST ever outside ride today. I did everything you said! Thanks!
-Linda UT

Don, I just wanted to thank you again for your clinic in PA. For me, the clinic was 10++. I now have a clear vision of where I am going. It never occurred to me that horses would have stages of progression and regression as they learn. Thank-you for that little tidbit of understanding! I never heard or saw anyone break down the canter and lead changes into their individual ingredients. It all makes perfect sense. I am trying to incorporate all that I learned into my daily interactions and play sessions. I'm anxious to show you the progress we're making. Thank again for all your help!
-Ellen PA

Thank you for your support. As always, it was an exhilarating time and so much to play with and think about! after! Thank you so much!
-Martha RI

I began coaching with you soon after my kids were born, thinking I would become a good natural horse trainer and enjoy hanging out with my friends. Little did I know I was really going to discover strategies that I would use in all areas of my life. I would never have guessed where my horsemanship would go. What I recognize, and want to honor you for, is that your coaching has such a broad view, that you have encouraged me to take advantage of every opportunity that has presented itself. You have continually kept me looking ahead. In the face of big barriers and big disappointments, that frankly would have stopped the progress of most people, you have helped me find ways to move on. Thank you. Your style is unique in that I have never felt pressure to conform, even when I feel I might be moving away from the base that brought me into the horse business in the first place, and I really appreciate that.
-Michelle VT

About Don Jessop

As an animal behavior expert, Don Jessop has been teaching and training leadership skills for the past 20 years in two unique industries. First, in the horse industry. After years studying behavior science with the best in the field, including: Pat Parelli (Natural Horsemanship), The late Ray Hunt (Horse Master), Ceasar Millan, (The Dog Whisperer) Lynn Eisenhart (World Class Dolphin Trainer), Anthony Robbins (Peak Performance Coach), T-Harv Ekar (Secrets of the Millionaire Mind) and more unnamed here, Don has mastered the skills necessary to deal with negative behavior, in his words "the emotional brain".

Don's skills have been called on by Olympic riders, peak performance coaches, and everyday people from all over the world. What he teaches are the skills necessary to train the *people* and their animals to reach their own goals and break through fears and limitations.

Don and his wife Rachel have traveled through every state in the United States and also England, New Zealand, and Australia teaching leadership courses and horsemanship mastery classes.

"I owe it all to the people who walked before me and the people who walk with me now. It seems even when I think I've got it all together I'm reminded how we can't do anything alone." Don Jessop

Made in United States
Troutdale, OR
06/01/2024